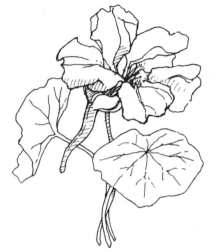

Gardening and Beyond

Gardening and Beyond

by

Florence Bellis

with illustrations by

Valerie Willson

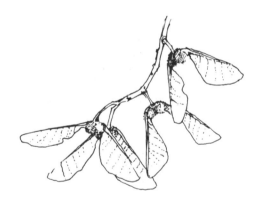

Nature and Artifice: Two Sides of the Gardening Coin
Volume 1 of the Series
Richard L. Critz, General Editor

DAVID & CHARLES
Newton Abbot • London

© 1986 by Timber Press
Illustrations © 1986 by Valerie Willson
All rights reserved

Printed in Hong Kong
Designed by Sandra Mattielli

First published in Great Britain
by David & Charles 1987

Bellis, Florence
  Gardening & beyond.
  1. Gardening
  I. Title
  635.   B450.97

ISBN 0-7153-9048-1

David & Charles Publishers
Brunel House
Newton Abbot, Devon

Contents

This book rounds off my life's work and my legacy
to all gardeners
in celebration of the beauty and bounty of the earth.

1

Dining on Dimes

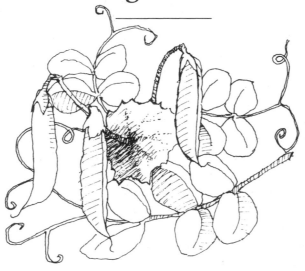

Too many of us have fallen into the habit of taking the plain and the familiar for granted. We accept the gifts of the well-known casually or with no thought at all until perhaps one day we discover some uniqueness in them, something new to us. So it was with me and peas and beans. They changed the face of my garden and opened my eyes to the unseen wonders of our planet working night and day to support us.

I had embarked on a money-saving, space-saving, soil-saving program and began by planting the tall varieties around rhododendrons and other shrubs. There they made their climb into the branches and dangled their pods in the sun. And after the picking, the roots of the peas and beans shed their protein-rich inhabitants into the soil and fertilized the shrubs in return for the support. The short varieties I planted near flowers and other vegetables to help feed them after they had fed me. In this way I learned that we are not asking of our soil all that it is willing to give us. And then I learned a great deal about giving to the soil and those who live in it.

With the need for farsightedness pressing us, I believe we can no longer afford to look at the soil as just something to walk on or as the medium that feeds us. I think the time has come when we must understand by what means we are being fed so that we will waste nothing that can feed in return. Not all of us know that our soil is the home and workshop of myriads of infinitesimal beings who prepare the bulk of the food our plants absorb through their roots. That among them are certain workers who recycle used food from organic wastes while other workers are busy converting fresh supplies of nutrients from inorganic elements of the earth and air. Because our continuing existence depends upon them and their work we cannot allow ourselves to be blinded by their invisibility.

These unseen creatures live in highly specialized family groups which have no need of us when they work at their own pace in nature. But gardening is not a natural condition. We expect beauty from the beginning to the end of the gardening year. We expect abundance from the vegetables we plant as seeds in the spring and put on the table in summer and fall. Yet how many realize that, in the ultimate analysis, the final preparation of the soil food that provisions this beauty and abundance falls mainly on the shoulders of these families. When these invisible workers become as real to us as any life we can see, and we start giving them the understanding and care we give to all living things, then, working together, we can bring from the earth food and flowers beyond believing.

The size of your plot is not important. By looking around your garden for spaces not used and spaces you thought were being used, you will find numerous possibilities for productiveness. My piece of earth is close to the sea, so close that the gulls sail over it like white kites on a windy day. It measures 100' square with most of it taken up by a sprawling old house and too much lawn. A few years ago this was a poor place supporting for the most part huckleberry brush and salal and blackberries native to this strip of Oregon coast.

I first built a garden that gave me only flowers. Soon I expanded it without expanding my space by growing vegetables among the flowers in such a way that one helped the other. It was then that I began making deliberate use of the unique power of peas and beans to leave the soil richer after they fed me than it was before.

I am not an amateur gardener. For some 30 years I was a mail-order nurseryman wholesaling and retailing plants and hand-pollinated seed throughout the States and overseas. I specialized in primroses only and won fame in both hemispheres for my Barnhaven strains and originations. I simplified and advanced methods of hybridizing and seeding that are now used as a matter of course here and abroad. Yet I am not ashamed to admit that I had to become a home gardener before I fully realized the wealth of help willing to work for me in my piece of earth. Here there is time to read and take things apart, to walk the beach and put them together again in simpler terms and relationships.

I studied some of the laws of Nature which seemed written primarily for scientists and educators. These riches lie there in their textbooks like dormant seed, seed too heavily coated with scientific language to let the flowers emerge in the layman's garden. Yet it is the home gardener who stands to benefit so handsomely in the business and beauty of living by knowing how all life, above and below ground, is interwoven for the survival of one another.

These earth laws, rooted in majestic simplicity and economy, take us to the very heart of conservation and the beginning of life as we know it. They show us with sudden clarity what to do and when to do it, the reason for doing it or not doing it, and all that a garden can be. It makes no difference where you garden, or whether you are just starting a garden or have been working the soil for as long as I have. And, strangely enough, it makes no difference whether you garden the total organic way or supplement with inorganic fertilizers. The laws governing survival on this planet offer guidance to all gardeners regardless of experience and conviction.

Know, first, that however much or little land we have, we own for the time it is in our care infinitely more than the soil we see and the plants growing in it. With our piece of earth comes a piece of the universe. "He who owns the soil, owns up to the sky" has been the law since man first settled on a parcel of land and called it his own. It extends from bedrock to the sky as far as the eye can see even to the stars we cannot see. It embraces the clouds which send down nourishing elements with the rain and snow and lightning; it enfolds the energizing rays of the sun. The very air we breathe supplies the basic materials our plants must have to manufacture the proteins that build and sustain their bodies and ultimately our own.

Meanwhile, in the soil of this self-contained little realm of ours, minerals are being reduced to their simplest chemical form for our plants to absorb. But, to me, of all these wonders the greatest are the families living under our feet unseen and unsung as soil bacteria. There, in their mute midnight world, they work and multiply and die in the fulfilling of their assignment to perpetuate life. It is the duty of some to provide a never-ending flow of unused, inorganic plant food from the elements of our planet. Once the plant absorbs this inorganic food it becomes organic. And once the food becomes organic, it is the duty of other soil families to recycle it from the remains of the dead and the residues of the living back to its original inorganic form for use again.

At first it was hard for me to understand that my plants could not absorb the food in the organic waste I returned to the soil until after the soil families had recycled it back to its original chemical form. It was equally hard for me to accept the fact that certain fertilizers, synthesized in factories, energize those families of the soil who must first convert its solid food content to simple, soluble elements before they and the plants can assimilate it. Then I learned how we—in our applied science—and our soil families and the weather, all utilize the same planetary elements to produce virtually the same kind of plant food in practically the same way.

If we could nourish ourselves as the soil families nourish themselves and the plants, starvation would be wiped out for all time. But we cannot draw sustenance from the nitrates and other chemicals these families convert from the air and mineral rock, and recycle from organic remains and residues. We must wait until our plants absorb these simple elements and then, in their own wondrous way, change them to the complex proteins, carbohydrates, minerals and vitamins that sustain all red-blooded life. This continuing flow and change from lifeless elements to living tissue and from living tissue back to lifeless elements is part and parcel of our natural world. Like a jade bracelet there is no beginning or end, for the beginning is the end and the end is the beginning.

I call this whole infinite scheme, so delicately integrated for the survival of earth life, the Master Plan. It is at once the heart and the lifeblood of what we call conservation. Conservation is the reiteration of the life process in which we all must take part. Just as each member of each soil family works in a waste-free society, so we should work toward that end. These families taught me the oneness of all life. I found that the one-celled bodies living below ground are powered by the same universal laws that power the myriad-celled bodies living above ground. That the need for air, food, water, and shelter is the same for the one-celled as for a cat or a queen.

With these vital needs of life in mind, I realized that organic material left in the rough, unrefined state of humus serves the soil families better than when it has been refined to compost. We all know that organic material is everything that once lived or was associated with life and that it contains, in

varying amounts, the nutrients used by that life. We also know how elegant compost is in its velvety blackness.

But this very fineness tells us that the soil families have completely recycled the organic matter to a state of total decay, and that the food it contains is now in soluble form. This means that if the finished compost is not distributed without delay, some of the nutrients will drain away into the soil beneath the pile while some will drift back into the air. But the major loss is the coarse fiber of humus which holds more air and moisture, and insulates against heat and cold for maximum shelter.

Humus is organic material that the soil families have not yet completely recycled. It is at the halfway point, midway between raw waste and finished compost. Its brown coarseness tells me that the food in it is still locked in insoluble form. I know that when I lay it at the feet of my plants as a mulch or lightly work it into the soil, the specialists among the recycling families will release its nourishment within root reach without loss to my plants. The unturned humus pile duplicates Nature's simpler process of providing soil life with its vital needs.

With Nature's total conservation in mind, I must say that the nitrogen we waste by not recycling our urine is staggering. Urine is the aristocrat of organic nitrogens, a product carrying urea metabolized from used protein. When the families who recycle nitrate from humus are all but paralyzed with cold in early spring, the ammonia in urine restores their energy. They quickly change the ammonia into fast-feeding nitrate and hormones, fresh and untainted, and hardly turn a finger in the doing. But the trick for us is to use it without seeming to use it. The neighbors do not know that when I make my rounds on chilly spring mornings after frost danger has passed, all is not water in my watering can. That more than half of it is urine.

Yet they marvel at the growth my plants make, at their health and the earliness and abundance of bloom. They also marvel at the size of my roses, and the glow on their blooms and the gloss on their leaves when roses would rather live inland than this close to the sea. Then I think how strange it is that in these frank times we shy off the subject of urine when the Victorians used it openly and discussed it freely among themselves and in print. In *Aunt Judy's Magazine* of the early 1880's is *The Little Gardener's Alphabet of Proverbs* for English children. The twenty-third proverb directs the young beginner to "Water your rose with a slop-pail when it's in bud, and you'll be asked the name of it when it's in flower". Even so, I felt shy about using it until I read that Agatha Christie's grandmother in Ealing attributed the size and beauty of her roses to the same liquid.

What I have done here in little more than three years others can do in less. This is a beautiful but difficult place to garden. At this moment the sea stretches before me like a blue prairie with mile after mile of white flowers blooming on it. But more often than not the winds are strong and you can almost taste the salt on them that they pick up from the sea. And the sun butters everything lightly but with an intense hand for here no impurities filter its rays and they burn like the salt on the wind. My soil was rock-hard yellow clay. Now it is black loam.

That first spring I dug down to the hilt of my digging fork, straight and unslanted for the deepest possible thrust, and turned up chunks of clay. I pounded them into the smallest lumps that I could, breaking two handles in the pounding. Then I spread over the clay a light coating of dolomitic limestone (a natural mineral deposit sold under the name of Dolomite) knowing that its calcium and magnesium would pry apart the gluey particles. Over the dolomite I spread an inch or two of small sharp rock for air and drainage. I next worked everything together, from top to bottom, and gently watered it to dissolve the dolomite. I then lightly worked in whatever humus I could find. The second spring I dug past the hilt of my fork and smashed the lumps—much smaller and workable now—and added the humus I had accumulated.

Then I learned where to plant to outwit the wind and everything grew better and provided more material for the humus pile. Before long the soil allowed me a choice. I could turn the humus under or I could lay it on top. Either way, the underground families multiplied in the humus and recycled more food than they could use. As the food increased the plants naturally grew faster, produced more humus material which, in turn, produced more recyclers who produced still more food. And so, round and round.

There seemed no space for vegetables until one day, after considering the high-priced produce losing flavor in the beautiful displays, I came home and took a really thoughtful look around. By then I had become fascinated with peas and beans. Like all plants that encase their seeds in pods, peas and beans house on their roots a remarkable family whose job it is to make the seeds rich in protein and then leave the soil more fertile when they die.

This absolutely indispensable family takes nitrogen gas from the air as it filters through the soil and converts it to nitrate which is their food. Part of this nitrate they trade to the peas and beans for some of the plants' excess sugar. In combining the sugar and nitrate, they produce protein and store it in their bodies. Meanwhile, the peas and beans are producing protein from these same materials and storing it in their seeds. When the plants' work is done and they die, the roots shed their residents into the soil. There, most of the workers die and the protein they made from atmospheric nitrogen and plant sugar is recycled back to soluble plant-feeding nitrate.

I first planted climbing Telephone peas and Kentucky Wonder beans around 10 rhododendrons, the flowering plum, and the Japanese quince. I planted the seed as close-in as possible for climbing support yet with an eye to the future sun needs of the young plants. Two half-circles of beans were planted on the sunny side of the bare-trunked oriental quince that postures in the wind-protected courtyard. The first was sown about two feet from its base, the second a foot farther out, staggering the seeds in their semi-circular rows. On the sunniest side of the most wind-sheltered rhododendrons outside the courtyard, I planted more beans. Around the purple leaf plum and the rhododendrons brushed with wind and shade, I planted the peas.

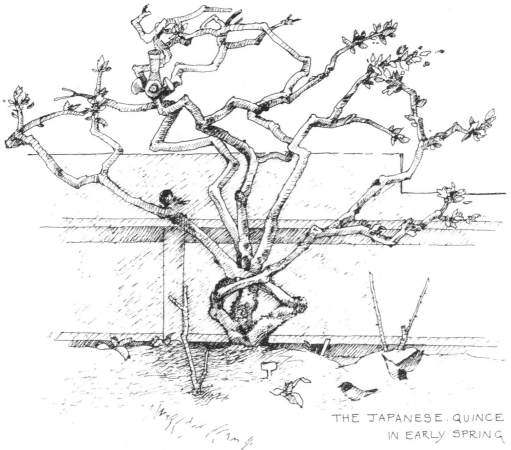

THE JAPANESE QUINCE
IN EARLY SPRING

The slender bamboo stakes, pushed into the soil and slanted up into the branches for the climbing tendrils to grasp, soon disappeared from sight. A solid front of leaves, blossoms and pods advanced to the shrub tops where the vines stretched themselves in the sun. The peas using a 14 foot native rhododendron for support could reach the lower branches without stakes. All the way to the top they looped their vines from branch to branch and dangled their pods like ornaments on a Christmas tree needing a stepladder to take them off. When the last pea and bean had been eaten I cut the vines for the humus pile and for mulch. But I left the roots to shed their inhabitants in the soil and fertilize the rhododendrons, the quince, and the purple leaf plum.

On the street side of the courtyard fence facing east is a strip of soil almost three feet wide. Against the fence is a long row of roses, and in front of the roses are English daisies—the old Bellis perennis because I like them and we share the same name—and among the daisies are clumps of wild iris and violets from the meadow nearby. Behind and between the roses are daffodils and a few double primroses. Among them all grow small lettuces, green onions and a few other salad things. In an exposed area to the north I sowed bush peas which turn their thick-leaved backs on the wind. A second planting there and a third elsewhere kept peas on my table well into the fall.

I next eyed the Japanese iris border. It is 40 feet long with three feet of soil separating the iris from the west lawn. For two years white petunias fluttered there like giant moths, but I was now seeing a great deal of beauty in vegetables. I had on hand some marbley farm potatoes and decided to buy two packets of bush beans and two of carrots to go with them—a $1.90 outlay. I faced down the tall iris with a row of potato marbles, three to a hole. In front of the potatoes I planted a row of bush beans. And in front of the beans, a row of carrots and let their feathery foliage sweep the lawn.

The potatoes in their swelling plowed and aerated the soil around the matted roots of the iris and around the beans. And the beans, maturing first and vacating their leaf space, helped feed the developing potatoes in back of them and the carrots in front of them as the spent roots dropped their occupants in the warm summer soil for recycling. For every three potato marbles planted I gathered seven or eight large and medium ones with enough new marbles to plant next year's crop. The beans and carrots I picked and pulled in tender youth. All were crackling crisp and sweet with the taste of the earth still in them. I had stopped nibbling on dollars and was dining on dimes.

But such good things as tree fruits and melons and sweet corn cannot mature here five blocks from the beach. And I would gladly forego a crop of peas to see tomatoes hanging ripe on the vine. Fortunately tomatoes do well indoors and I always pot up a few in the spring, leave them outdoors in a sunny, protected spot until early fall when I bring them in to the west bay window. There they continue to bloom, pollinate themselves, and set fruit which I pick, red-ripe and juicy, throughout the winter when tomatoes are an unaffordable luxury.

Strawberries, on the other hand, grow wild and sweet here. Next spring I will buy 25 of some everbearing variety and plant them among daffodils and hyacinths in a wide sunny bay sheltered from the chilly northwest wind by a broad curve of rhododendrons which, in turn, are protected by tall Scotch brooms. By the time the berries form, the daffodils and hyacinths will have been picked or, fading, cut for the humus heap. Should the bulbs' leaves take more than their share of the sun, I will tie them up for that short time it takes them to sink back into the earth again.

There are two sheltered areas waiting for a promised pair of artichokes whose leaves, deeply cut and dusted with silver, were designed to trap the rays of the sun. I can see places for Brussels sprouts here and there among the carnations. And I will plant a few zucchini and crookneck squashes where they can sprawl, while in smaller spots I will plant more spinach for steaming as well as for salads. In the larger spots the sun and wind will decide whether it will be bush peas or bush beans. All of this I will do and report on.

I wish I could find the words to tell you what my plot of earth means to me. Perhaps we must discover for ourselves the primitive satisfaction of growing food in the unused spaces of our garden without compromising its beauty. But I will say this. We have in our yards what many countries would consider a wealth of space but, because we are so used to spaciousness, we accept it without much thought or gratitude. In a small but gratifying way I feel part of the whole when I return to my soil what I take from it but cannot use and when, later, I receive more because of the return. This of course is simply old-fashioned thrift. Yet it goes back farther than that. Ever since life first appeared on this planet Nature has been using and reusing everything, wasting nothing.

JAPANESE QUINCE ~ LATE SUMMER

2
The Miracle of Our Unseen Help

This morning is unusually warm and windless for January. The sun and low tides have brought the woodcutters to the beach and for two days now I have heard the whine and drone of the saws slicing driftlogs into rounds. Only a short time ago these giant remains were fir and spruce and hemlock living in the forests of the coastal mountains. The flooding rivers carried the fallen ones down to the sea and the sea tossed them back on the land like so many matchsticks.

The sun has also warmed the soil of my garden and wakened the families living in it. It has brought them back to the work they dropped when the earth first chilled at the thought of frost. Some of these families are more important than others, but even the least among them are needed to complete the hub around which the Master Plan revolves.

The greatest family of them all is the one called the bacteria of decay. I think of them as our housekeepers—more precisely, our earthkeepers—for without them we and all that live on the land would suffocate in our own leavings. Without them, organic wastes would pile higher and higher in a Frankenstein nightmare. It is this family that shoulders most of the responsibility for recycling the remains of life and the wastes of the living first to humus and then to compost.

The housekeepers have set their alarm for 37° F. They like much warmer soil, doing their best work in the upper 70's to middle 80's. Yet at 37° they have wakened and, slow-paced with cold as they are, doggedly start breaking down plant and animal remains. They energize themselves with the sugars and starches and other essentials in the organic matter they are recycling. And when they have reduced the identifiable material to fiber, they have reached the halfway point of their work. They have recycled raw waste to that reservoir of life substances—humus, humus in the soil and humus in the heap.

In the humus are all the nutrient elements that the raw waste contained. These nutrients too are only at the halfway point. For though the housekeepers release the nutrients, they leave them in their complex insoluble form which the plants cannot use. It is then the job of the specializing families to reduce these compounds to their simplest chemical form. So the sulfur family picks up the freed sulfur and recycles it to soluble plant food. The phosphorus family recycles the phosphorus. And the protein has been freed to start retracing its steps back to nitrate.

Humus protein, once it has been released by the housekeepers, is turned into amino acid by enzyme action. The amino acid is taken up by the ammonia-making family which turns it into ammonia for the specialists who will follow. These specialists are the nitrifying families. The nitrifiers work more swiftly than the ammonia-makers for as soon as the ammonia appears, the nitrifiers snatch it up and in two adroit maneuvers recycle it back to the nitrate that feeds them and the plants.

Unseen by the naked eye but very real, each soil family has its own habits, its own degree of mobility, its own beauty of color and form. Down the ages each has followed its own underground star. To whatever mysterious beat the nitrifiers move, they move with unwavering precision. Two families are needed to take the two steps from ammonia to nitrate. Both families are master chemists. One takes up the ammonia, releases its hydrogen content of three atoms, then replaces the hydrogen with two atoms of oxygen, no more or no less.

This changes the ammonia to nitrite. But plants do not use nitrite. Just as soon as the first nitrifying family completes the preliminary step, the second family picks up the nitrite and adds the one more atom of oxygen needed to transform nitrite into plant-feeding nitrate. In Nature's hands, atoms are the cosmic seeds of life.

When seen with seeing eyes, the perfection of the Plan inspires the utmost humility and reverence. Its economy is without flaw and its harmonious interaction makes mismanagement impossible. It sees that the nitrifying families are there working in the same temperature range as the housekeepers and the ammonia-makers, and in ratioed numbers. And that whatever the range, working cold or working comfortably, they all work in unison, never quitting.

There is ecstasy too in this world of theirs. When the soil is moist and airy and rich with humus, and the sun waxes warm and the earth answers, the families flare into a frenzy of excitement. Faster and faster they divide in the moist heat and with the food and the air, multiplying with each dividing. Faster and faster they work as their numbers soar astronomically in the upper inches of the soil drawing part of their energy from the sun yet wanting protection from its direct rays. Then when the soil's richness ebbs, or when it cools or dries, their numbers fall and their bodies enrich the land. Their ecstasy, like ours, cannot be maintained.

But while the excitement is upon them, they can recycle humus protein to nitrate in a few weeks. Where the soil is seldom warm, or when air and water are not in comfortable amounts, it takes them years instead of weeks. Where there is no warmth, no air or no moisture, there can be no recycled nitrate for these families cannot live there.

The amount and kind of fertilizer that our soil families produce for us depend upon what we do for them and upon the weather. It makes no difference whether we put our leavings directly on the soil as a mulch, where it will be recycled to humus, or on a pile to be recycled there before transferring the humus to the soil. If the waste contains feeding substances in wide variety, and is kept moist, the housekeepers and the specialists will set an ample and well-balanced table for themselves and the plants in the warm times.

But in the cold times when recycling is slow there will be little, if anything, left for the plants. The soil families, being the provisioners, sit at the first table and the plants at the second. And even when food is plentiful the plants will still go hungry unless their roots can reach it. The soil families have some slight power of movement and can undertake a restricted search for food. But plants must stand in one spot and hope to survive on whatever comes within root reach.

Since the earth was in its first greening, plants have been able to take up their soil food only in liquid form. To this end the housekeepers recycle solid food to insoluble compounds, and the specialists recycle the compounds to soluble chemical components. Only then, when the nutrients are in their simplest elemental form, can they dissolve in the soil water—that watery film that clings to the soil particles. There, around these moist specks of earth, the plants wrap their silvery root hairs and absorb their food and drink.

Too often our humus piles are not in good balance. We tend to look after a plant's nitrogen/nitrate needs but overlook the others. So our waste material is often oversupplied with nitrogen and undersupplied with phosphorus and potash and the other nutrients needed for productivity and health. I think this is because we all know that nitrogen is the most important of all the nutrients, that it is the growth food and without growth there can be no life. Yet unchecked growth defeats the aim and purpose of life. Phosphorus and potash must be there to steady and strengthen growth and make it productive. A deficiency of these two regulators causes plants to grow and grow either delaying maturity or preventing it.

Maturity is that quiescent period in the life of so many plants when they flower and seed but do not materially grow. This is their nuptial time and all their growth and development and storing of food has been made in preparation for it. They advertise their need to procreate in color or fragrance, or both, luring pollinating agents to penetrate their blossoms for the nectar within. For every kind of flower there is an agent—ant, bee, moth, butterfly, hummingbird—all eager to probe for the nutritious nectar and, in the probing, consummate conception. However, if plants cannot flower in their true season for lack of phosphorus and potash, their reproductive period can come to nothing. And if they have been pushed too fast and too long with nitrogenous food from any source, their growth is spindling and weak. They have been robbed of their stamina and are powerless to resist disease, pests, and the extremes of weather.

Nature dispenses nitrates with a judicious hand and eye to balanced growth and timely maturity. She does not overfeed, and to guard against underfeeding she has empowered two families to make fresh supplies from the air. These families are called nitrogen fixers because they fix, or stabilize, atmospheric nitrogen to nitrate to feed themselves and the plants.

Both nitrogen-fixing families are stationed throughout the world. But only one has made a gentleman's agreement with peas and beans and other

pod-bearers to exchange nitrate for sugar. We cannot see them without a microscope but we can clearly see the homes they make for themselves on the plants' roots. The fixers enter the young plant by way of its hair roots and work their way up to the main roots where they induce clusters of nodules. They then settle down in these warty swellings—ranging in size from pinheads to marbles depending upon the host plant, its age, soil, and weather conditions—and start converting unusable atmospheric nitrogen to usable nitrate.

This nitrogen family leads all others in the production of nitrate because their source of supply is unlimited. Every breath we take is almost 80% nitrogen. So when air circulates freely in soils growing pod-bearing plants, these nitrogen fixers contribute anywhere from 80–250 pounds of nitrate annually to an acre from the protein stored in their bodies. But while they lived, they made it possible for their hosts to produce high protein seeds. Of these, peanuts, soybeans, lima beans and lentils are the highest. One cup of shelled peanuts provides 39 grams of protein. This is 50% more than any treeborne nut supplies and almost equals the protein in half a pound of roast beef. One cup of soybeans provides 22 grams, dried limas 16, lentils 15. In comparison, one egg supplies 6 grams.

NITROGEN NODULES

The summers here are too cool to mature soybeans and limas but both prosper wherever tomatoes ripen. On the other hand, lentils do well here as they do in northern Europe where they were a staple some years ago, perhaps still are on small farms. They should do well in all average gardens. Each pod carries two lens-like seeds and when picked, shelled and steamed at once, have a delicious meaty taste. I have found no source of lentil seed other than the packages I buy for soup but they give me total germination. Lentil foliage is lacy and low, about a foot, and is pleasing in the landscape.

That peanuts are limited to southern climates is a serious loss to northern gardeners. The vines take from four to five months, even longer, to ripen their seed and they cannot stand hard frost. A few northerners grow these tender annuals for their showy yellow flowers (whose pollen fertilizes the plain, unnoticed flowers blooming at the same time) and to watch the strange way the seed pods bury themselves. After pollination, the infant seed capsules find their way into the earth just as an infant marsupial instinctively finds its way into the mother's pouch and, there, matures.

The peas and beans and lentils that I grow, and all the other pod-bearing plants in every part of the world, are members of the great and powerful Pea family. There are more than 12,000 species in this family, classified as legumes, and though they all carry their seeds in pods, here the family resemblance often ends. They differ strikingly in habit of growth and shape of bloom just as all widely distributed families—both green-blooded and red-blooded—differ in color, size, and other physical characteristics as a result of adapting to their environment over a long period of time. There is no plant family more widely scattered than the legumes. They range over all the plains and semideserts of every continent, in the forests of both temperate and tropical zones, on land rich and poor. Only one or two plants outside the Pea family offer their hospitality to the nitrogen fixers. Here it is the alder tree.

The legumes are an amiable family. There are vegetables and flowers for every climate and every garden asking only average growing conditions and care. Many require no care. Some of the shrubs and trees excite the senses with their graceful ways and alluring fragrances. The Redbud tree starts pulling pink lace over its winter-naked limbs early in the spring. And the Rose-Acacia, swinging its bunches of pink sweet pea flowers, lavishes a heavenly scent on every breeze that passes by. Then there is the flowing grace of the laburnums and the feather-form leaves of the locusts with their aphrodisiac perfume. And the temple incense of the Wisterias, elegantly oriental. And for warmer climates, the true acacias embodying eternal spring with the unforgettable fragrance of their little pompons, fluffy and yellow as baby chicks.

These are but a few. My stand-by on this windy hill is Scotch broom. Though a European, it has naturalized itself along the Oregon coast where it lives with the wind like a native. As a newcomer here, arriving in an idyllic September, I knew nothing of the summer wind that springs out of the northwest too many mornings at precisely 11 o'clock, stays all afternoon and sometimes into the night. When I found that I had planted nine of the young rhododendrons directly in the wind's way, I planted brooms behind them in a widely curving arc. They were little more than whips when I dug them from a broom thicket. Today they are two and three inches through at the base rising to a windbreaking twenty feet. In August their dry seed pods click in the wind like castanets. In May their bloom-burdened boughs of yellow and bronze and almost-pink sway ponderously over the rhododendrons now in their own splendor of bloom.

These and all the other rhododendrons averaged around three feet when I planted them. Now they have more than tripled in height and width though I cut trusses for myself, my friends, and for hospital rooms from March through June depending upon variety. Yet they are not slowed by the cutting. Nitrate feeding has been left entirely in the hands of the soil families. The nitrogen fixers contribute their bodies when the climbing peas and beans die, and when the brooms slough the fixers off with their old roots. The recycling families process the nutrients from the fixers' bodies, the lawn clippings I mulch with, and the leaves and blossoms dropped by the rhododendrons themselves.

The other nitrogen-fixing family does not lead a cloistered life on the roots of legumes and alders. It lives free and easy in the soil of quiet places and is the lesser of the two because its members are naturally lazy. They take no thought of the morrow never caring if they have one atom of their own to rub against another. They have the same unlimited supply of atmospheric nitrogen that the cloistered family has but, because they live free in the soil, they are not dependent upon it. They much prefer to sponge off the recyclers' surplus nitrate until the supply dwindles and competition forces them to fix their own from the atmosphere's gas. So they contribute only 10–40 pounds of nitrate to an acre in a year, a modest donation in comparison to the cloistered family's but important to the land with no legumes on it.

These free-living nitrogen fixers congregate in soils left undisturbed for a number of years, or not disturbed at all. They leisurely work the meadows and pastures, and such places as old deserted gardens and graveyards where the flowers have long lived without attention. I know several such tranquil places. Snowballs and lilacs, peonies, iris and roses abandon themselves there after half a century of neglect—islands of color and fragrance in a land where the rain falls only now and then.

In my nursery days I sought relief from the spring surfeit of primroses and color and rain by driving east over the mountains to the dry part of Oregon. Barnhaven was not on the coast. It was 100 miles inland on the dampish western skirts of the Cascades. This great Cascade Range with waterfalls never counted divides the wet western third of the state from the two-thirds of the dry. Every year in late May or early June I took a handful of weeks and crossed the mountains. There the vast hot stretches dried my skin and warmed me, and the monotone distances drained my eyes of color stored up. I lost myself on the high plateaus that are central and eastern Oregon, drifting without thought or plan along unfenced wheatlands and grasslands, through deserts of juniper and sage.

But first I visited friends who have lain so many years now in the crumbling graveyard beside a crumbling pioneer church. These old friends were gray-haired and sitting tired in the saddle when I was not yet 20. The roses covering them and the lilacs shading them were brought across the Plains by their mothers before Oregon was a state. Yet after all these years Nature is still embroidering more roses on their coverlets.

Then I would ride as in the old days, fast at first to feel the warm wind on my face before letting the horse pick its way in its own time across Juniper Flat and White River Canyon. On the other side of the canyon was a deserted homestead which I had come upon years before. The old two-storied house, like the church, could scarcely be seen through the yellow roses. Each year I marked on my mind how far the roses had climbed until they covered the walls and finally the rafters' boniness. The whole place was wallpapered in yellow roses with only a board here and there left showing for the years and the weather to rub satin smooth and silver.

No hand tends these plants whose fragrance drifts deeper into the lungs there in the semidry than here in the wet. The old Austrian Coppers and Harrison's Yellows, the yellow climbers and prairie roses, the snowballs, lilacs, iris and the great crimson globes of the peonies are all watered by the snows that come early and stay late, and by the chance thunderstorm of summer. They are fed by the recyclers living in the soft, scented duff of fallen leaves and petals, and by the nitrogen fixers drawing nourishment from the sugar in the petals and from the nitrogen gas in the air.

Cherish these families of the soil. Call them bacteria if you like since no better name has yet been given them. Lump them all together as microorganisms since their numbers are beyond counting. Diminish them, if you will, for the soil upon which you stand, if it is fertile soil, lodges in one small spoonful more than all the people in the world. But know that in their mini-universe they are Davids engaging Goliath. Cherish them for your life is inextricably linked with theirs.

3
Home and Weather Contributions

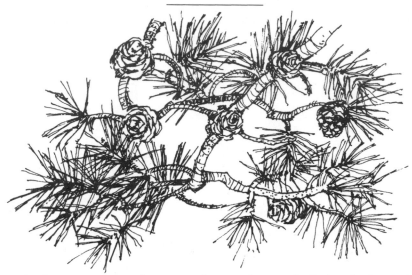

A pine grove guards my garden on the south. In its shady middle the pines grow straight and tall and in their reaching for the sun entangle the southwest wind. This is the showery daffodil wind and it melts the snows when they come out of the east. At the sunny edge of the grove where my garden begins, the pines have so relaxed their limbs they seem part of an oriental painting. With finished grace their angled branches frame the primroses and violets beneath them and partly screen the humus heap in back.

My humus pile is as much a part of my garden as the flowers I love and the vegetables that are my pride. It will become part of my soil and my soil is an atavistic part of me. It is a simple collection of pullings and sheddings, cuttings and parings which measures some 50 feet long, averages about 3 feet wide, and a low 2–3 feet high to let in air for the recycling families. It is not in deep shade nor is it in full light. One-half the length is humus ready to use. This ripe half, last year, was raw garden debris and kitchen waste which I kept moist but did not turn. This year's raw half will become next year's humus. Thus the halves alternate.

As I use it I restock. When the soil mellows in the spring I turn it over with a digging fork and lift out the weeds. The soil has dried enough to shake easily from the roots of grass, chickweed, and other unwanteds which I carry to the raw half. From the ripe half I carry back the humus, mulching the flowering plants and forking it under where I will soon plant vegetable seeds. With the spring digging I also release the winter's accumulation of stale air and bring a rush of fresh to the soil families and the roots of the plants so that, once again, all can breathe freely. With the humus I bring food to the soil families who set to work at once in the warming, freshly aired soil to recycle it. And with the weeds and grass, food for the coming year is being stored up.

As the summer and harvest progress so does the raw half of the heap. There are carrot and potato tops, pea pods, spinach and lettuce roots, and the spent vines of peas, beans and lentils whose roots stay in the ground to shed the last nitrogen fixer. Then there are the faded flowers, and old bouquets, and all the flowering plants that could not keep themselves within their appointed bounds. As I lay them on the heap I am sad that they must end this way—calla lilies, montbretias and foxgloves, hardy fuchsias, daisies and native violets, and the legendary Ladders-to-Heaven we know as Lilies-of-the-Valley trailing romance in the wake of their unforgettable fragrance.

I say that my humus pile is simple only because I let it take care of itself. But no hand turns the fallen leaves in a wood or the dying grasses in a meadow. Actually it is a mound of complex chemical mystery which still baffles men. We know that the housekeepers are there leveling the recognizable to the unrecognizable. That they are reducing it to fiber and water, carbon dioxide and mineral compounds, readying the protein for its journey back to nitrate. Yet only the soil families themselves know exactly how they do it.

In the mound, also, is packaged energy that the plants took from the sun when they lived. There are acids, by-products of the recycling process which help break down the insoluble mineral compounds to soluble chemical nutrients. It is a lifeless-looking mound teeming with life and it healed the sick soil I found when I came here.

Humus is the great protector of the soil and the life in it. When the recyclers have finished their work and the food it contained is part of the soil water, the humus particles attract and hold most of these feeding elements against the downward pull of gravity. And when the rain beats the earth the humus softens the blows and keeps the soil from packing hard and blocking all the air lines to plant roots and soil families. When the summer rains do not come it tempers the soil and keeps it moist. In the cold months it traps the rays of the weakened sun. It supports my plants when the high winds circle the pines and brooms and find a way in. And where I found but five scrawny blue earthworms when I first dug this neglected soil, they now tunnel and aerate, eat and excrete in pink plumpness everywhere.

These virtues round out my reasons for preferring rough brown humus to refined compost. Synthesis now duplicates the recycled nutrients in compost with inorganic nutrients to such an extent that they are one and the same to plant life. But we cannot duplicate humus whose physical properties bring health and well-being to the soil and all its inhabitants.

I started putting my lawn clippings and those of my neighbors around the rhododendrons when I first planted them because there was little or no other organic material on hand. The airy layer of grass kept the soil moist in summer and returned to humus before next spring's heavy mowings began. There is no reason now why the clippings should not go on the humus heap except that I am in the habit of it, a step is saved, the peas and beans get mulched, and the rhododendrons could not be in finer fettle.

In progressively bolder steps I have passed on to the housekeepers all peelings and other raw kitchen waste. At first I discreetly put them in an old ten-gallon bucket and kept it in the warmest out-of-sight corner I have, covered loosely to admit air. After every four or five colanders of waste I dusted it over with dolomite. This sweetened the waste which pleased the housekeepers who recycled the contents in warm weather almost as fast as I could supply them. It also added nutrients that would eventually please the plants.

I worked this odorless mush lightly into the soil around whatever needed a boost. The bucket method saves the nutrients in the leavings and the face of the timid gardener but loses the humus. So I began taking the kitchen waste to the humus pile where I hid it under the garden litter. Soon I was scattering it on top. Now I spread the bulk of it about an inch below soil surface throughout the garden, between rows or plants, starting at one end of a plot and methodically working toward the other. The less obvious pods and tops, along with spent flowers, I lay on top of the soil as a mulch.

My fireplace ashes I use with discretion remembering that heavy or frequent applications can throw the soil off balance. But the potash and

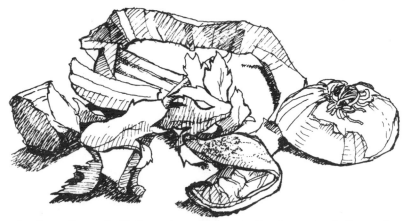

calcium in the ash, and all the other elements the trees took from the soil in the years of their growing, work wonders when used in moderation. I lightly scatter some on the raw half of the humus pile since the soil families like its modifying influence on the recycling acids. Every year or two I work some into the soil around the roses. At the same time I work some into the soil where vegetables will be grown but never near rhododendrons which, to a variety, pale at the very thought of lime which the ash carries in quantity.

These are the ashes of oak logs delivered to me from the Valley, and of bark that the sea stripped from the drifting spruce, fir and hemlock and cast up on the beach. When I gather the thick slabs and haul them home and warm myself before their ultra hot blue flames, cooking over them when the wind downs the power lines, my pioneer days seem not so far away. An earthy contentment settles over me. It is the feeling of self-containment which deepens still further when I return the remains of the trees to the earth that bore them.

Early flowering perennials, such as primroses, do their feeding and storing in late spring, summer and fall after they bloom, but are quick to respond in early spring to any fast-acting nitrogen which acts as a stimulant. Consequently an unexpected freeze will, almost certainly, destroy the bloom—even the plant—if leaf growth is encouraged too soon. All liquid nitrogens, including urine, and solid nitrates should not be given until new leaves appear after flowering. Since the majority of spring flowering primroses keep their leaves over the winter, growing in every mild period, I believe it unwise to give them, or any other early blooming evergreen plant or shrub, nitrogenous fertilizer after August no matter what form is used. Let

THE PINE GROVE ~ EARLY SPRING

26

the recyclers take over with humus nitrate which automatically tapers off as the soil cools, safely shutting off entirely before frost.

Late spring and summer blooming perennials really do appreciate an early urine lift but only after temperatures stabilize above freezing. Many of these are herbaceous and the early spring growth, so very tender, should not be stimulated too soon with immediately available nitrogen. Even a fairly light frost can wipe off new growth which has been induced against the better judgment of the plant.

Herbaceous perennials which bloom in late spring and summer have two feeding and growing periods—one in the spring before they flower, the other after they flower until frost or their natural rhythm brings dormancy. Though I give them urine in the spring before they bloom, after they bloom I almost always let the recyclers supply the nutrients for their late summer and early fall growth. Fall flowering plants, such as chrysanthemums, have one long uninterrupted feeding and growing season beginning in the spring and continuing until they bloom. I pass them by.

Plants have individual temperature preferences in which they do their best, but collectively they start growing when the soil warms to around 41° F. But at 41° the soil families have been awake for only 4°, are sluggish with cold, and can recycle only enough food for themselves. Surplus begins to build only when the soil begins to warm, but until the soil is truly and constantly warm the plants have a lean time of it. Yet nitrogenous food in the early weeks of a plant's growth, after the last frost, is as necessary for a vigorous start as protein is in the life of a child. Without it, both have difficulty catching up with the better fed. To me, urine is the most logical head start food. In addition to supplying vital needs, it is always safe in dilution, always on hand, costs nothing, so why buy a lesser product.

In the past, Europeans and Asians commonly used urine and solid human wastes (called night soil) on their harvest land. Some countries still do but I use urine only on my ornamental plants. Yet we use all kinds of animal manure on our food plants and never give it a thought except where to get it. The soil families have to recycle all organic matter, which naturally includes urine and manures, to its original chemical elements before the nutrients can dissolve in the soil water and be reused by the plant. Nevertheless I do not use or advocate using urine on garden produce. In countries where private wastes are still being used, the inhabitants apparently thrive on the fruits and vegetables that backfire on visitors.

The watering can I use for diluting urine holds nine quarts. I use about two-thirds urine to one-third water knowing that organic concentrates of any kind, insufficiently diluted, can damage plants as quickly as inorganic concentrates. My love for roses sends me to them first. I pour a full can around each bush to reach the deepest feeder roots, and in a circle wide enough to supply laterals. Of course this is done after frost when I prune, since pruning in itself promotes tender new growth.

After the roses I do the fuchsias which so far have over-wintered here though the top growth has been wiped off a time or two in a surprise severe freeze. The Japanese iris usually come next and they truly leap, being among the plants preferring ammonia to recycled nitrate. They use nitrate as well but there is a reason for their preference. Ammonia takes a firm grip on the soil and does not wash away quickly like nitrate which takes no grip at all. So Nature seems to have given plants originating in wet climates and marshy places this added insurance and they still cling to their ammonia habit even in gardens much less wet than their homeland.

The phlox and carnations come in for a share if circumstances permit, and lilies of all kinds benefit indirectly since they are planted alongside and amongst almost everything. But I make sure that the roses get another can apiece and they give me blooms from late May through most of the summer and fall. Even in mild winters they trickle along. I have just brought in 10 stems, some in bud and others in frightened January bloom.

This usually ends the program for the year. The earth is warming, the soil families are warming to their task, and the plants have had their head start. If I made a practice of using urine when soil temperature gets into the 80's and humus nitrates are plentiful, I could be forcing growth at the expense of bloom. Yet when I could not resist giving the roses an extra can or two in July after their first flowering, their second flowering in August, September and October was a splendid sight. Leaves and stems were a shining mahogany, flowers glorious in matching health. In the courtyard, in borders east and west, everything and everyone bathed in their fragrance, charm and individual beauty. I counted 119 buds and blooms on one floribunda. It was a vision in purest pink and every bud and bloom was an exact replica of the silk roses I so loved on my mother's Edwardian hat.

To these homely, often wasted organic fertilizers, the weather adds inorganic fertilizers in its more dour moods. Rain and snow bring some 5–10 pounds of ammonia to the average acre during the year. Some of this escaped the nitrifying families and drifted back into the air, but most of it is a combination of atmospheric nitrogen and hydrogen. Lightning deposits around 11 pounds of nitrate each year on an acre where electrical storms are moderate, much more where they are intense. This is a fusion of atmospheric nitrogen and oxygen which falls to earth as nitrite where it converts to nitrate.

Men eventually realized that they could take these same atmospheric elements and, to all intents and purposes, duplicate the weather's products. They first produced nitrate by passing nitrogen and oxygen through electric discharges which simulated lightning. Shortly after, they combined nitrogen and hydrogen gas from water and solidified it into ammonia crystals knowing from past experiments that rain, distilled, condenses into a crystalline ammonium powder. They knew that when this product was scattered on the soil and scratched in that the nitrifiers would convert the ammonia to nitrate when the soil was moist and warm. They also knew that these inorganic nutrients, like those produced by the weather, would become organic once the plants absorbed them and transformed them into living tissue.

Ten days have passed since I first heard the woodcutters cutting drift logs in a warm January sun. And for 10 days the soil families have been working in the rare warmth. I have cut roses and fuchsias, picked primroses and pink violets. Now I am suddenly aware that I did not hear the whine of the saws this morning when the tide was low and that I am cold. I look up from my work and see that it is beginning to snow. I leave the desk and stand awhile watching its quiet falling darken the day. This evening I live in a Japanese print. The pine branches are tufted with snow. Beneath the branches and the snow the primroses and violets bloom and the soil families sleep.

4
Surprising Facts About Organic Fertilizers

It is hard to believe that in this computer age there are many who still remember when animal manure was an unquestioned fact of daily life. We remember the street cleaners in white with their scoop shovels, brooms and handcarts in the city, and sidestepping it in the country. We still laugh remembering those lazy farmers who pitched it out the barn window and let it stack up until it clogged the opening. And we now know that few, if any, of the tidy farmers who carted it out to their fields to get rid of it and to improve their crops knew exactly why it did. Even today few home gardeners know that unconsumed organic material carries more nutrients than after it has been ingested, digested and expelled.

More than 2,000 years were spent trying to discover the life pattern of plants, 2,000 years of striking matches in a sealed cave. All that time men searched for the answers to such questions as: what is their food, how do they eat it, how do they grow, how do they reproduce without the visible means of animals. Aristotle believed that soil was the food of plants as well as the stomach and small intestines—that the soil particles were predigested by the great soil body before the plant took them up and distributed them to all its parts without forming wastes.

No one seriously opposed Aristotle's doctrine until the 17th century when a Belgian challenged it for the first time with an experiment instead of words. Using a boxed willow tree he proved to his satisfaction that water was the sole food of plants, that soil only kept them from toppling over and tempered heat and cold. Later in the century an Englishman, experimenting with mint, proved to his satisfaction that soil was indeed the nourisher of plants and that water served only as the carrier. There were those who claimed that air was a plant's total food, others that it was the "essence of fire". Then Jethro Tull stormed in.

Tull was a London barrister and organist who left city life against his will in the early 1700's to manage one of his father's farms in Oxfordshire. He put together the world's first seed drill more to relieve himself of dissatisfied laborers than to advance agriculture. It was a product of his musical past built of organ parts and parts of two other instruments. He next invented the first cultivators to prove his plant feeding theory—2 and 3-pronged implements so heavy and unwieldly that it took three bullocks to pull them.

Tull's chronic anger and ill health must have grown out of coping with farm problems when he preferred music and law. He lashed out at all who differed with him, particularly those who disagreed with his plant feeding theory. He was convinced that soil, pulverized to microscopic particles, was the food of plants and that his cultivators were necessary to pulverize and press the particles into the plants' sucking root-mouths. Once in the mouth, the plants passed the particles on to the root-guts where they were digested and the wastes defecated. He considered manure of questionable value. It helped the cultivators break up the clods but it also brought weeds which competed with the crops for the soil particles.

Tull died in 1741 and before the century was out the farming gentry was discarding Tullian agriculture along with Chippendale pieces and other things of which they had tired. The "old Chips" drifted out to the cottages and farmhouses on the estates where too often they were chopped up for firewood and burned with cow manure picked up from the fields and kneaded together with straw. The gentlemen farmers were appalled at the waste of manure because they had embraced the fashionable new humus theory. But since not one common farmer in 5,000 could read—according to a contemporary agricultural writer—they followed in the footsteps of their forefathers though the path often led to hunger and despair.

Actually there were two humus theories. The original was founded on the misconception that plants took carbon from humus and through some mysterious vital force transformed it into minerals. Not everyone thought that minerals were necessary for plant growth, and those who did considered them stimulants, not nutrients. The second humus theory dropped the idea of vital force, and after further modifications seemed so logical that many still believe in it. It has been handed down from generation to generation as my mother handed it on to me. The modern humus theory holds that humus is the food of plants. And that plants extract the humus and minerals from the soil in combination with water and transform them into tissue.

In 1840 science overthrew theory. In that year Justus Liebig, a German who was the leading scientist of the world, in his book, *Organic Chemistry in Its Applications to Agriculture and Physiology,* shattered the prevailing humus theory. In it he presented his own agricultural findings and those of other scientists which, individually and collectively, stood every test. The results never varied. And though it was published in eight languages, the facts were too revolutionary for popular acceptance. Few could believe that living things in the soil brought about the decay of organic wastes. Equally fantastic was the revelation of how plants feed, the nature of that food, and the chemical composition of manure.

Liebig, still in his thirties, was also an angry man. His anger sprang from the prevailing stubbornness that would not accept proven facts, and the wastefulness of the German farmers. He was a driven man, yet he left his work from time to time to go among the farmers and exhort them to gather up all animal and human wastes and spread it on their fields. I like to believe that our farmers of that period were better husbands of the soil though virgin land was theirs for the taking. Certainly the farmer who keeps animals today is loath to part with any manure for town and city gardeners. But this works no hardship on us since farmyard manure is more practical for the farmer than it is for home gardeners.

The manure of most farm animals is low in feeding elements even when it is fresh. And when it has aged sufficiently to come in contact with roots without burning, most of the nutrients have drained away with the urine seeping into the ground beneath the pile, and by the ammonia escaping back to the air. The farmer can catch the urine in tanks or in the animals' bedding which if it is hay, or even straw, carries a higher nutrient content than the manure itself. He can sheet-compost this urine-impregnated bedding and the fresh manure by spreading it on the land he is resting, or on land he intends to plant in the coming months. But by the time the manure is safe enough for the gardener to work into his soil, it is mostly fiber.

This may be hard to accept since home gardeners have long looked upon animal manure as the ultimate in organic fertilizers. But though the plant nutrients it contains are small, the value of the fiber is great. The latter guarantees air, holds moisture, shelters roots and soil families, and conditions the soil—cow manure binds light soil while horse manure loosens heavy soil. I believe that the fertilizing aura surrounding manure expanded with the garden club movement which the Ladies' Garden Club in Athens, Georgia started in 1891. As clubs spread throughout the country, gardening and manure became fashionable. Then the garden books and garden magazines, following in the wake of the garden clubs, all extolled the nutritional virtues of manure.

Actually the average humus pile contains twice the feeding elements of an old manure pile. Soil families, recycling organic matter in the humus pile or in the mulch or in the soil, leave more food than they take. Animals, in digesting and assimilating vegetable matter, use practically all the nutrient content leaving a bare minimum in their solid wastes for the soil families to recycle. Little was commonly known about the nutritional value of humus and compost until Sir Albert Howard, working in India, published *An Agricultural Testament* in England in 1940. It became the springboard for the organic gardening movement started here in 1945. Since then, humus and compost have steadily gained in esteem. Yet an odor of sanctity still clings to horse and cow manure.

I believe that their low nutrient content is directly related to environment and body functions. Dairies and horse farms usually locate where grass is lush and green. The high water content in the forage dilutes the food content and encourages further loss by frequent urination. Moreover, the dairy cow is either carrying a calf or giving milk and in need of all the nourishment she can extract from her food. Fresh horse and cow manure contain considerably less than 1%, each, of nitrogen, phosphorus, and potash—the three primary plant feeding elements.

On the other hand, steer manure carries 2% nitrogen, $+\frac{1}{2}$% phosphorus, and almost 2% potash. It varies, but this is the analysis on the sacks I am currently storing. The higher nutrient content in steer manure, and the trace elements it is reputed to carry, reflect an austere environment and no reproductive responsibilities. Steers manage in drier regions where dairy cows cannot. For quantity marketing they are usually raised where summer forage is yellow with the dryness, so food concentrates in blade and leaf. There is little water anywhere so there is little urination. Such regions also contain minerals not found in lush areas, and these the steer takes up in its feeding. Add to this the grain fattening in the feed lots where the manure is sacked.

Often the build-up of a product is followed by the letdown of scarcity but, like the manure of old, sacked steer manure is everywhere. Garden shops and supermarkets all sell it in moisture-proof bags which store easily. It is then on hand when needed and there is no nutrient loss as with bulk manure. It is odorless or carries only enough to confirm its origin. It is weed-free. And though I always use it when planting ornamentals it has never burned. I mix perhaps 6–8 quarts with soil and humus in a large hole for a large shrub or smallish tree; around 4 quarts for smaller ones. Perennials get several double handfuls mixed into each hole. When it is forked into vegetable plots with humus, the combination works wonders. It is well to read the contents listed on the sack before buying to make sure that you are getting steer manure unmixed with a useless filler.

Chicken manure is high-powered because chickens cannot urinate. The ammonia that animals void in their urine concentrates in the droppings of fowls. Straight droppings deliver 4% nitrogen, 3% phosphorus, and 2% potash. Its high nitrogen content requires two warnings—it can burn roots on contact, and it can make leaf at some expense to flower, pod, and root. Even when the droppings come mixed with litter, it is wise to mix them with peat moss or soil and then work the mixture about an inch or two into the soil surface and water it in. Chicken manure, like urine, should be used only in the spring after frost danger has passed, or in early summer.

Users of rabbit manure consider it superior to chicken manure. They get it either from rabbitries or have it produced in their backyards since more and more gardeners are keeping rabbits for the dual purpose of food and fertilizer. I know a Shakespearean actor who keeps a pet rabbit for its droppings. He built a hutch for it over his half-hidden humus pile and there the pellets keep falling on whatever kitchen and garden waste is not fed back to the rabbit. His garden is small, a revolving wheel of flowers and food, and always he claims the first ripe tomato in town. Though rabbit manure's nutrient content is only half that of straight chicken droppings, its 1½% phosphorus and +1% potash seem to effectively balance its 2% nitrogen which gives steady growth without risk of stimulation.

Sheep manure is valuable for its 2% nitrogen, 1% phosphorus, and 2½% potash. But lucky is the owner of a goat. I once fell in love with a Nubian who was the sole companion of an old mountain woman. When the day's work ended the goat was invited into the kitchen where it sat beside the old woman in her rocking chair and together they enjoyed their evening gumdrops. These gentle creatures not only give milk and clear land, they produce droppings which carry almost 3% nitrogen, 2% phosphorus, and 3% potash because they prefer to browse on leaves than to graze on grass. However, leaves do not have to go through a goat to provide plants with a highly nutritious diet.

Autumn leaves drifting on the wind mean different things to different people. Some delight in their beauty. Some see only the need to rake. Others appreciate the phosphorus and potash and other minerals in them which help balance the nitrogen in their humus pile. Every living thing must have phosphorus to strengthen its structure. In plants, phosphorus strengthens trunk, branch and root; transfers and stores food for the making of flowers, fruit and seed. It contracts the expanded, watery cells of the plant that has taken up too much nitrogen, toughening its tissues so the plant can withstand winters it could not otherwise survive. It is phosphorus which intensifies color and sheen by increasing substance where thinness was; which encourages early maturity, and puts richness in the fruit.

Yet our soil carries so little of it. Only where many men and animals lived and died and mixed with the soil is the soil naturally rich with the phosphorus that once strengthened their bones. Nor is phosphatic rock likely to be in our soil for it mainly concentrates on the fringe of warm seas, and those parts of the earth where the seas were in ages past. This is so because the phosphorus in such rock is the fossilized remains of fish and other sea animals imprisoned there so many millions of years ago that their bodies mineralized to inorganic elements.

Potash has its own way of reinforcing phosphorus. Long recognized as the developer of roots, its other powers reach deep into a plant's being. It helps in the making of sugars and starch which fruit, root and pod crops need in greater quantity than leaf crops. It promotes cell growth in stem, foliage and fruit, and bolsters during drought. It increases the plant's capacity to resist disease, and encourages vigor and good spirits when days have long been without sun. It works hand in hand with phosphorus in helping the plant avoid collapse when temperatures sharply drop.

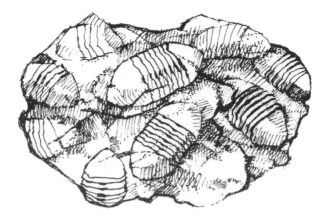

Potash is the everyday name for potassium. It stems from the old practice of burning wood in pots and working the ash into the soil. Some primitive earth-scratcher evidently noticed that where fires had been, his crops were better and reasoned that it was the ash which made it so. Slow growing hardwoods, such as oak, contain up to 10% available potash when unleached by rain. Fast growing softwoods, such as fir, hemlock and spruce, may contain less than 2%. All wood ash is high in calcium compounds and lime, sometimes as high as 40%.

The sea has always been the earth's reservoir of minerals and their chemical components. She stores millions upon millions of tons of potassium alone in her body. And on some pieces of land that once knew her are billions of tons still to be mined. It is in the rock particles that are part of our soil, but the weather and soil acids must first break down the particles before the mineral can be released to soluble chemical form. So plants could well be starving for potassium in the midst of rock-bound plenty.

We cannot hope to add much phosphorus or potash to the soil with bottled or boxed organic fertilizers other than bone meal. If the product carries more than 2% each of phosphorus and potash it is usually inorganic. Fish emulsion is the fertilizer commonly bottled and it is mostly nitrogen. The boxed meals offered in the garden shop here are entirely nitrogen— blood meal 9%–12%; fish meal 10%; cottonseed meal 6%.

Organic products are always labeled organic. And the law requires that the percentage of available nitrogen, phosphorus and potash which a product carries, organic as well as inorganic, be prominently displayed in that order so that buyers know what they are getting. We all know that N is the

THE GARDENING CORNER

symbol for nitrogenous fertilizers in its various forms, and that *P* is for phosphorus. But few know that *K*, the symbol for potash, is the first letter of *kalium,* the Latin word for potassium.

Plants can absorb the nutrients in liquid fertilizers in a matter of hours. At most they are in the soil no more than a month. They should be used as I use urine—once or twice in the spring when temperatures stabilize in the 40's. The habitual use of nitrogenous concentrates can become a dangerous practice. With the rapid greening and growing it is easy to forget the needed phosphorus and potash and humus with its fiber. Soon the plants, high on quick nitrogen, will show their need for a balanced diet and a healthier way of life.

Added to the temptation of using fast-feeding nitrogen too often, too early and too late, is the danger of using too much. Labels warn about the possibility of burn and it is wise to use less than the minimum amount recommended. It is also wise to use it in the morning or evening, not in the warm part of the day, and then only after the soil is wet from watering or rain. If the plants you intend to fertilize have yellowing leaves, first check the soil for drainage in the spring and moisture in the summer.

Plants fly the yellow leaf to signal their need of air or water much more often than they do for nitrogen. Packed soil is common in the spring, especially after a wet winter. What it needs instead of fertilizer is a good deep cultivation and humus, and perhaps rock chips, to open it up and let the stale air out and the fresh air in. Plant roots, like us, take in oxygen and expel carbon dioxide. As the roots deplete the supply of oxygen in the soil, carbon dioxide builds and the plant literally suffocates. In summer the plant with yellowing leaves is pleading for water. It is not only thirsty, the soil needs water to dissolve the nutrients already there, and to supply the sun-powered, cosmic production of a good 90% of the plant's food by way of its leaves.

Meals require warm, moist, airy soil—and time—for the housekeepers and specialists to release their nutrients. They provide nothing in cold, dry, or waterlogged soils. When conditions are favorable nitrogenous meals are recycled within a few months, but it is a different story with bone meal. Soil families take from 1–3 years, sometimes longer, to make available the 11% phosphoric acid content in the finest grind of raw bone. Steamed bone naturally recycles in much less time, carries approximately 15% phosphorus, and because it is more readily available needs replenishing more often.

Perhaps a note should be made about bone meal's alkalizing tendency. It may not be enough to worry about but you may want to keep it away from plants originating in woodlands, high rainfall areas and other wet places which are accustomed to acid soil. Among these are rhododendrons, azaleas, heathers, camellias, chrysanthemums, Japanese iris, ferns, most of the lilies and all of the berries.

In the first half of the 19th century English farmers relied heavily on crushed bone. But they did not know why it benefited crops in some locations and not in others. Nor could they understand why crops dwindled when springs continued cold. Nevertheless, their demand for bones was so great that Liebig accused England of removing every year "the manural equivalent of three millions and a half of men" from Europe's battlefields after the Napoleonic Wars. And, furthermore, that she had sacked up generations of skeletons lying in Sicilian catacombs and crushed them for fertilizer.

We did not need to use the bones of men for bone meal. After the Civil War, when we turned our attention to taking the Great Plains from the Indians, we slaughtered the buffaloes as the quickest way to reach this objective. They were richer bones than those of the European soldiers for the buffalo had eaten well because he always returned to the soil more than he

ate. For countless years the great herds had cropped the green and golden grass and gave back its richness with their residues and remains. They matted the grass thickly over the fertile prairie lands we coveted. And in their final death they gave to the soil the last of their flesh and all of their blood. But their bones were gathered up and stacked in mountain chains alongside the newly laid railroad tracks.

Decades before we started using buffalo bones for fertilizer, Europe's bone reserves were gone and virgin land was a forgotten dream. Her population was increasing and her decreasing farmlands were producing less instead of more. In 1842, out of Liebig's work and out of necessity, John Lawes ended agriculture's dependence upon bone. He was a quiet young man, in his twenties at the time, and so obsessed with plant nutrition that he used his manor lands near London for experimental research. There he found a way to produce readily available phosphorus from fossilized phosphatic rock which approximated the phosphate in bone. Crops then flourished in all soils and all locations, and in the cold months as well as the warm.

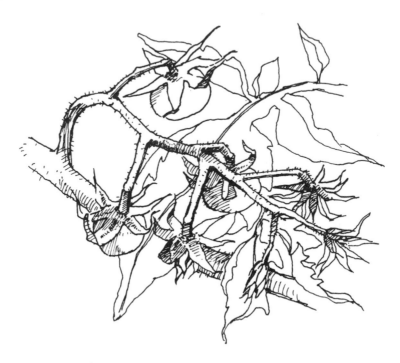

5
Inorganic Fertilizers: Their Unique History and Use

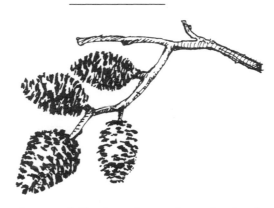

Nurserymen who specialize in only one branch of a plant family carry all their eggs in one basket. If they trip they have little or nothing left to sell. This is particularly true when their plants are evergreen and winter-active and the weather shuttles back and forth between freezing and growing temperatures. The grower soon learns that if he is to stay in business he must sleep with the weather night and day from mid-fall to mid-spring. Even then he can be deceived as I was together with a forlorn number of rhododendron and strawberry growers that year of the debacle in the Pacific Northwest. Had we hardened off our crops before the freeze with phosphorus and potash, total loss may have been averted. But no. The horse had already been stolen before we knew enough to lock the barn door.

Indian summer lingered long that fall embracing everything with false promises. The strawberries in the fields and the rhododendrons in the nurseries grew on in tender leaf. My primroses, growing in an old apple orchard on a hill facing the mountains, had so abandoned themselves that you could not see the soil. The snow peaks had stripped to their last patch. Then, overnight, the mercury dropped some 50 degrees. There was no snow to cover the leaves and buds hurrying toward premature bloom with never a thought of disaster.

The dairy manure I had wrongly used as a winter mulch between the rows was from the loafing sheds and ran heavily to urine-soaked straw. This warmed the soil still more and every shower leached ammonia. As the plants grew on, their cells enlarged with water. So when the freeze struck, ice crystals formed in the tender, water-swollen leaves and crowns. The crystals, drawing upon this water, collapsed the cells and rot set in. This is how plants winterkill.

The rhododendron and strawberry growers who escaped crippling damage had hardened off their plants with a newly marketed liquid formula sold under the trade name of Liquinox 0-10-10. Produced only in California, it is mostly distributed on the Pacific Coast so has little more than story value for most gardeners. It carries no nitrogen and its 10% phosphorus and 10% potash, both inorganic, are carried in a yucca base. Wise growers used this product 2–3 times during that fateful fall. The roots absorbed it quickly from the warm soil, contracting the cells of all top growth, as though a series of frosts had occurred, which made the plants more or less inactive.

Gardens can be hard on plants, especially winter-active/early-blooming ones originating in environments where Nature provides protection. Either the winters are mild or they are snowed in where winters are severe. Or the plants grow in light woods and meadows where fallen leaves and grasses lightly cover them, or snow falls in freezing periods to shelter them. And where nitrogen intake slows with the cooling soil. The winter-active plant is so pitifully vulnerable in vacillating climates when leaves are exposed to sun and wind in freezing temperatures for any length of time. Or when a sharp freeze suddenly strikes during a mild growing period and there is no snow covering.

Here on the Oregon coast the temperature sometimes drops without warning into the low 20's abruptly ending the make-believe summer. But I have never forgotten the lesson learned at Barnhaven so, toward the end of October, I use Liquinox 0-10-10 on the primroses, roses and fuchsias. Another application is given about three weeks later even though I keep evergreen boughs or other non-packing material on hand to cover the primroses when the soil has frozen. This, of course, does not help gardeners in areas outside the Pacific Coast but there must be substitute products within easy reach.

Dry phosphorus/potash combinations, without nitrogen, such as 0-10-10 or 0-20-20 should be available. If there is a choice I suggest 0-20-20.

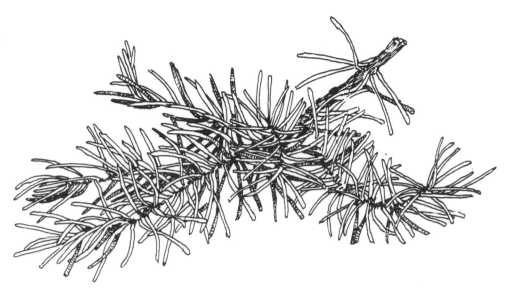

Phosphorus from rock moves relatively slowly in the soil and some of it locks back to unavailability until weather action and soil acids break it down again. If such nitrogen-free products are not available there is always superphosphate which carries 18–20% phosphorus but no potash. I have never heard of superphosphate being used for hardening off but there is every reason to believe that it would do so. Though the feeding elements in treated mineral rock are water soluble and readily available, I doubt that the phosphorus and potash can be taken up as quickly as in liquid form. This indicates an earlier application, perhaps September or very early October depending upon past weather patterns. It is advisable to use less than recommended, keep it off leaves and crowns, water in well after lightly cultivating or perforating it in.

The phosphorus and potash a plant takes up in the fall does far more than help it survive the winter. The roots store it until spring when it is used to balance nitrogen, to stand guard in a freeze, and to strengthen the plant when it first begins to grow. If the humus pile could supply phosphorus and potash without nitrogen I would use humus. But, of course, this is impossible. Nitrate always predominates over the mineral content in humus. In any event, the cooling soil would prevent recycling in sufficient amount and as quickly as needed.

Those who rely on untreated phosphatic rock get very little from it even over a long period of time. Before phosphorus can be released into solubility it must be broken down by harsh treatment from the weather—alternating freeze and thaw and rain—and by soil acids. These forces working together finally reduce the mineral content to its chemical components, but it is a slow process which yields only negligible amounts even in strongly acid soil. In slightly acid and neutral soils it is practically worthless because the rock comes from the mine in triple calcium form which must be reduced to its double and single forms before any nutrient release can begin. Acids used in treating rock for ready availability are essentially the same as acids in the soil which bring about slow, natural breakdown.

Acid carries a bad image but it is inescapable. The soil contains sulfuric acid, phosphoric acid, nitric acid and others. Sulfuric acid is a corrosive liquid made by combining sulfur, oxygen and hydrogen and is the one most commonly used to treat phosphatic rock. In the soil the sulfur family produces sulfuric acid using the same materials—sulfur, oxygen and hydrogen. Contrary to popular belief we need not fear a sulfur build-up in the soil when using treated mineral rock. Sulfur is a nutrient of vital importance to plants in producing protein, furthering other functions, and favorably influencing all nutrients. Some of it is neutralized by the soil's electrical charges. And, like nitrates, it is highly mobile and passes quickly through the soil.

When John Lawes first experimented with sulfuric acid on crushed bone before moving on to phosphatic rock, circumstances were weaving a disaster pattern in Europe. The Napoleonic Wars had been over long enough to double the population but the increase in food production was still alarmingly slow. When Liebig was born in 1803 it took nine European farmers to support one city family in addition to their own families. The industrial revolution was taking men away from the farms who, with their families, consumed food they did not produce. So the farmlands, already near exhaustion, were asked to provide quick turnover crops which rapidly stripped the soil of humus and recycled nutrients. And the hands that could have restored fertility with sufficient organic matter were working in the cities.

Lawes' 1842 patent for superphosphate included several other so-called patented manures he had been working on. He was so immersed in his work that he gave no thought to the long and grueling hours spent in research and labor to develop his products before manufacture and sales could begin. But success was marred by the disapproval of his family, family-to-be, and friends. They were horrified that he would even consider entering trade. And with chemical manures! Having to gamble practically all his assets to build the processing plant could not have helped matters. The venture brought him scientific renown and financial recovery but mixed with pain. His products brought lasting relief to agriculture's mineral problems.

Today's superphosphate remains essentially his process. It keeps the same name (he called it Super Phosphate to indicate the substantial 18–20% available phosphorus), and carries the same phosphoric content. The sulfur resulting from the processing and the calcium accruing from the fossilized remains in the rock counteract one another and have no effect on the acidity or alkalinity of the soil.

Liebig insisted that superphosphate and other patented manures should be used only in conjunction with animal wastes which he believed were the backbone of the soil. Patented manures, he said, should be considered supplements to animal manure and used in the smallest amount necessary to replace what the previous crop had taken from the soil. Today's farmers and vegetable gardeners who use superphosphate with humus or manure in the spring say that this combination of minerals and organic matter produces the finest crops in the shortest time.

When the home gardener uses superphosphate or any other processed fertilizer for vegetables or flowers, it is better to side dress, or band, the rows and individual plants. If the fertilizer is worked into the soil before seeding or transplanting there is always danger of burn when the tender young roots make contact. By working a narrow band into the soil alongside the young plants—with seeded plants after the first true leaves appear—the developing roots will intercept it in solution when they are able to safely absorb it. Start about 1½–2″ from the plants and make a band about an inch wide so scant that the soil is not completely covered. Slip a narrow trowel an inch or two under the band and turn it over in the same place like a pancake. The soil should be moist but not saturated when the fertilizer goes in, then watered well but not flooded.

Lawes' work with minerals did not preclude his joining others in hot pursuit of that will-o'-the-wisp—plant-feeding nitrogen. Elusive and frustrating, atmospheric nitrogen could not be captured and reduced to ash and analyzed like mineral solids. It was known that nitrogen is the main element of the air, that it is necessary for plant growth, and that manures and decaying vegetation provide it for plant use. But what was it that changed the ammonia in manure and decaying vegetable matter to nitrate? This question was argued up one side and down the other. Some were positive that it was chemical action while others were equally positive that it was biological. At the same time the extent of its need was being disputed, some, convinced of its need, were trying to unravel the mystery of legume nitrogen. Many of science's greatest minds teased this tangle of unknowns from Liebig to World War I.

These were the decades when the whole system of creation was unfolding before men's eyes like a rose unfolding its petals one by one. They worked with absolute singleness of purpose, giant contending with giant in the fields of medicine and agriculture for both held secrets in common. Liebig, Lawes, and Pasteur all defended their investigations with pen and tongue sharpened by conviction as they winnowed facts from theory.

Liebig and Lawes disagreed about the importance of nitrogen. Liebig based his argument on an experiment that he and his students had made with rainwater. Together they collected the rain in blankets—running with the wind toward the town to avoid pollution—distilled it and recovered sal ammoniac crystals. This led Liebig to believe that the ammonia he found in rain had escaped from decaying vegetation, which it does but in smaller part.

Though he had found nitrogen in every plant cell, he still thought that the ammonia from rain and decaying organic matter was sufficient to supply agricultural crops if minerals were replaced as used. Lawes based his argument on experiments he was making on his 250 acres at Rothamsted.

During this time Lawes endowed Rothamsted Manor as the first farm experiment station and it continues to disseminate information to farmers on a world-wide scale. In 1843 he took as his assistant Dr. J. Henry Gilbert, and their famous experiments with wheat proved that nitrogen was much more important than Liebig believed. But their search for the source of legume nitrogen, which lasted more than 40 years, took a wrong turn and, slight as it was, lost them the discovery of the nitrogen fixers.

Two German chemists, Hellriegel and Wilfarth, isolated the fixers in 1886 with experiments along the same lines as those of Lawes and Gilbert. They found that peas and lupines flourished in sterile sand when they added only phosphorus and potash and some of the soil in which these legumes had previously grown. By the process of elimination involving experiments with other leguminous and non-leguminous plants, they found that the young peas and lupines died whenever the potting soil, in which peas and lupines had previously been grown, was pre-heated to a killing temperature. This two-sentence account can in no way convey the magnitude of the contribution these two agricultural chemists made when they proved that living things inhabit and stabilize atmospheric nitrogen in those baffling nodules on the roots of leguminous plants.

Nine years before the nitrogen fixer discovery two French scientists had used heat to determine whether chemical action or biological activity changed ammonia to nitrate. They needed to know this before proceeding with their Pasteur-inspired but self-appointed task to make the discharges from the sewers of Paris safe for irrigating the fields around the city. They found that when long glass tubes were filled with soil and diluted sewage passed through it that the contents lost ammonia and gained in nitrate after 20 days. But when they heated the tubes to the boiling point, all activity stopped. Action also stopped when they permeated the tubes with chloroform—a Liebig discovery made before his preoccupation with agriculture. Then an exciting thing happened. As soon as fresh garden soil was added to the cooled and aired tubes, nitrate production resumed as though it had never stopped.

By this time the population had doubled again and people were

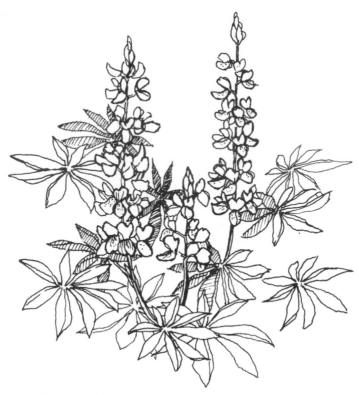

living longer. More food had to be grown on less land, and more men were flocking to the factories. There was no danger of running out of minerals. Sources of phosphorus-bearing rock were practically unlimited. And five years after Lawes and Gilbert proved, in 1852, that potassium was of primary importance to plants, Germany discovered that the ancient inland sea which once covered most of northern Europe had deposited, in one relatively small area, more than 20 billion tons. Nitrates were now the problem. The weather and soil families together could not produce enough nitrate even had there been the hands to keep the soil supplied with organic matter, and had every spring been warm enough to encourage speedy recycling. Oriental farmers had long solved their nitrate problem by storing and using urine from every source. For thousands of years all wastes were held sacred to agriculture.

Europeans had been importing nitrate of soda from Chile since 1820 but agriculture did not use it until the century neared its end. Nitrate of soda is a readily soluble, mineralized compound that the sea left behind eons ago in what is now the Atacama desert high in the Andes. This ancient marine plateau contains some 70,000 square miles of sea-deposited minerals, or did before mining began. Nowhere else in the world was there a worthwhile deposit of sodium nitrate, commonly called Chile saltpeter, and the Atacama supplied 95% of all inorganic nitrate being used until World War I.

Germany had stockpiled enough Chilean nitrate to last six months, an ample supply to see her to victory in a war she knew would be over in half that time. But after three months it became apparent that the struggle was not nearing an end and that a blockade now prevented her from bringing in more. She had to find a way to produce a never-failing supply of nitrate quickly and on the spot for future crops as well as explosives. Some of her scientists evidently were quick to see the effect lightning has on nitrogen and oxygen and that all they had to do to duplicate atmospheric nitrate production was to build factories that would funnel in air and pass it through electric discharges.

Shortly after the war—in the United States, I believe—atmospheric nitrogen and hydrogen were combined to produce ammonia which provided the raw material for a wide group of nitrogenous fertilizers. These are now in more general use than nitrates. Fossil fuels also contribute nitrogen for agricultural use but the search goes on for still other sources. Biologists are now attempting, by gene transplant, to induce the nitrogen fixers to live with cereal grains as well as with legumes.

In these ways men learned how to feed an exploding population crowding into the cities. But in doing so they created another problem. The soil families over-populate their own world when nutrients are readily available. Then when this easy food supply decreases to the point where it can no longer support their spiraling billions, they fall upon whatever organic matter they can find and literally burn it from the soil. As the recyclers deplete the humus and its nutrients, uncountable numbers die off for want of food and their bodies leave the soil richer for a time but poorer in structure. So agriculture's problem now is maintaining enough humus to protect the soil's physical condition while cropping the maximum.

Home gardeners sit in the catbird seat because each can decide for himself how he will manage his plot of earth. If he fertilizes entirely with organic material he knows that the soil families can recycle only the amount and kinds of food the material contains when the soil warms to working temperature. If he uses inorganic fertilizers he knows that he must provide compensating amounts of organic material for soil structure and health. But whichever way he goes he should never forget that air and water are absolutely vital to the production of at least 90% of the plant's food by leaf and sun.

I have had visiting well-wishers pull my weeds and poke my fire and I do not intend to make the same mistake by fertilizing another's garden. However, a few generalizations may help those confronted for the first time by the printing on inorganic fertilizer bags. All balanced, or complete, fertilizers carry the three primary feeding elements—nitrogen, phosphorus and potash. Other elements that accrued in the processing of the product, or from companion minerals in the rock, or were added to remedy mineral shortages existing in the region of sale, are also listed.

Each element's percentage of availability is prominently displayed on the label. For general garden use, choose the one with more phosphorus than nitrogen, and less potash than either. A combination such as 6-10-4 (6% nitrogen, 10% phosphorus, 4% potash) or something similar, can always be had. It is advisable to choose the product with a lower percentage of available nutrients than one with a higher.

Balanced fertilizers usually carry nitrogen in two or more forms. Most of them include water soluble nitrate for immediate use and ammoniums for recycling later when the soil warms. Some contain urea—which could be called synthetic urine in solid form—and it approximates ammoniums in recycling time and conditions. A few include urea-form which recycles slowly for up to eight months since it has been coated with resin to retard the recyclers' work.

The listed nitrogens should be carefully considered. If nitrates are part of the nitrogen content, the fertilizer should not be used until danger of spring frost has passed. Nor should it be used after mid-summer on perennials or flowering shrubs, particularly those keeping their leaves over the winter. Since ammoniums and urea are recycled when the soil is warm and moist, these products should not be used after mid-summer to avoid stimulating fall growth. If urea-form is included, calculations should be made as to what the weather will be like eight months after application.

Application instructions should also be carefully read and, more often than not, disregarded. Like all concentrates, less is better than the recommendation on the label and certainly they should not be used as often as suggested. I repeat that side dressing rows and individual plants is always safer than mixing the fertilizer with the soil before planting. For shrubs and trees, a very light scattering from trunk to branch tips (called the drip line) perforated in or lightly turned under is the wise course. And once again—always keep the fertilizer from touching leaves and crowns. When leaves touch the ground, bunch them in one hand and hold them up until the fertilizer has been worked into the soil. Always water in dry fertilizer well but do not flood it, and remember that it should not be put into dry soil. Nor should it be put on wet grass. And still again, belaboring a much-belabored warning—never underestimate what frost can do to nitrogen-stimulated growth.

For about a week after fertilizing it is well to check the plants now and then for signs of wilt or burn. Should this happen, immediately flood the soil to remove the nutrient overload. Under normal feeding conditions there is less food in the soil water than in a plant's roots, and the flow of nutrients from soil to roots goes on as it should. But when over-fertilizing concentrates more food in the soil water than there is in the roots, nutrient flow reverses and moves from roots to soil collapsing the plant. If noticed in time, heavy watering may remove enough excess fertilizer to restore normal osmotic flow.

As to how to run a garden I can speak only for myself. For one thing, not everyone shares my earthiness which probably is a leftover from my great-grandmother who was a peasant. She worked the wet Baltic soil of Pomerania in the 1840s and survived only because she wasted nothing that could be used again. And she held on to the bird in her hand instead of waiting for the two that might show up in the bush. Her typical peasant thrift and caution could be another hereditary leftover. But undue caution can be a crippling thing. Fortunately I dropped a significant piece of it on the beach one day when the pattern of planetary thrift came together for me and I lost my fear of the word *inorganic.* For the first time I could see the magnitude of the Plan wherein inorganic becomes organic only to return again to inorganic. I saw why everything on this earth must be used and reused over and over again without end for continued survival and to have a place to go.

It is never easy to change thinking habits when confronted with something that opens new vistas but two lines written on the sand opened the doors of my mind. I came upon them as the sun was setting one wonderfully warm evening in May. All the Sunday sightseers had gone leaving behind them their bits and pieces of empty words scattered on an empty beach. Alone, I read these lines written in the most beautiful calligraphy:

> *Do not reject what you do not understand*
> *for with understanding comes acceptance.*

I slowly turned and watched the surf curling and breaking on the shore. For the first time I saw how the curl of the slow wave is like the curl of the earth as it leaves the plow. But I was thinking about the words. Whose words were they. Who had etched them there with such infinite care knowing that the tide would erase them in a few hours. There was no way of knowing. Nor would the one who wrote them ever know how they blossomed in the mind of at least one who read them.

6

Forgotten Fertilizers

Calcium, magnesium and sulfur put muscle in a plant's limbs and roses in its cheeks but we hear all too little about what these three secondary feeding elements do for a plant's health and general well-being. Instead we are told at great length about the effect these elements have on the pH of the soil. As nutrients, calcium—the active element in liming materials—builds and strengthens skeletal structure. Magnesium helps manufacture chlorophyll and oils. Sulfur is vital to chlorophyll and protein production. Nature provides these minerals singly or in combinations tailored to the needs of both plant and soil. A garden can have it three ways at once when more is known about these silenced nutrients and use them to feed the plants at the same time they are conditioning the soil's structure and correcting the soil's imbalance if it exists.

So much talk about these elements as amendments has stimulated a preoccupation with the degree of soil acidity or alkalinity very like that of a hypochondriac searching for symptoms to treat. The pH (abbreviated from the French *puissance de Hydrogen,* or strength of hydrogen) is the measure or degree of hydrogen the soil is carrying. By now everyone knows that calcium and lime counteract acidity and some know that sulfur modifies alkalinity.

Doubtless the practice of testing the soil and adjusting its pH continues to be the thing to do and I am sure there are others besides myself who carry a certain amount of guilt for not doing it.

At Barnhaven I sometimes thought about it but could never take the time for it. Yet I grew successfully and in quantity members of the Primula family from widely differing environments and soils—woodsy primroses from England, leather-leaved ones from the alpine meadows of Europe, lush-leaved spectaculars from the southern slopes of the Himalayas, fuzzy-leaved and mealy-leaved ones from Japan, the Caucasus and the Mediterranean. I wondered about their complacency so far away from home and decided that some day I would put a few basic facts together and see if a pattern emerged. It did, and like every pattern in our orderly system it is simple and logical.

Nature cannot cater extensively to the individual preferences of her children, plant or animal, so all have had to learn to adapt to some extent. Always there are exceptions, but of the great number and diversity of our temperate zone plants the majority adapts to the average garden. A garden is average where rainfall is average. And average rainfall promotes an average soil influenced, of course, by the disintegrating rock upon which it lies.

In regions of high rainfall everything conspires to make the soil strongly acid. The lush vegetation with its dense root growth produces large amounts of organic acids. Herbaceous plants add their acid top growth and the evergreen trees native to wet regions drop their acid needles. Layers of this humus sink back into the earth every year to which the rain brings hydrogen with every fall.

It follows that low rainfall areas carry only a trace of hydrogen. Natural vegetation is sparse and small of leaf providing little humus. The rock base is usually limestone which supplies the vegetation with alkalizing nutrients so these are all it can return. Even the water is alkaline, "hard" as we call it, carrying as it does large amounts of alkalizing minerals.

Our high rainfall areas are usually narrow strips banding average country. Low rainfall areas are semiarid strips separating average country from arid regions. Growing in these high and low rainfall belts are plants that cannot change their need for acid or alkaline soil any more than plants coming from abnormally dry or wet regions of other countries. They belong to the minority which prospers because of the overages or underages of rainfall and related soil conditions. Some adapt to average situations when the soil is made more acid or more alkaline but they still miss the deluge or the drought.

The great majority of plants are content in our wide stretches of average country receiving a fair balance of rain and sun as the seasons turn. It is true that among them are those with soil preferences just as there are those with temperature preferences. But for the most part it is more preference than demand and a healthy soil with the proper choice of secondary nutrients can usually satisfy it. Most of the vegetables and ornamentals we grow have a much greater capacity for soil tolerance than is generally supposed. Without an easygoing adaptability, peas and beans—said to be intolerant of acid soil—could not produce as they do around my rain-loving rhododendrons which demand and certainly get acid soil on this wet coastal fringe.

Precise gardeners are probably happier knowing the exact pH of their soil and adjusting it to the degree of acidity or alkalinity decreed for the plants they grow. Casual gardeners, growing average plants in average climates, can be happy knowing that they need not concern themselves if they return to their soil plenty of organic matter that has been lightly dressed with wood ashes, ground limestone, dolomite, or other calcium-bearing materials.

Among our planet's life patterns none is more profound than the linkage of all land creatures to their forgotten beginnings in the sea. We still carry in our veins approximately the same proportion of salt and potassium and calcium as there is in sea water which, like our blood, is slightly alkaline. And for nine months we live in a watery world, not breathing, as we develop in preparation for birth and air. The phosphorus and calcium that harden the shells and bones of sea life harden our skeletons for we took the habit with us when first we left the sea. Every living thing must have calcium and its use and reuse revolve in a stately, slow-paced rhythm.

For eons calcium has been concentrating in the sea and in the bodies and shells of sea creatures from the microscopic to the mammoth. And for eons the sea gave great quantities of it to the land as she withdrew from the rising continents. With every withdrawal she left behind vast layers of calcium embedded in the shells and skeletons of the life she had nurtured. The ages crushed and cemented them together into solid foundations and great mountain chains of limestone rock. And, as in eons past, the rains keep carrying the calcium from the rock and the soil to the rivers, and the rivers carry it back to the sea.

Much of our country rests upon such a limestone foundation. Its formation is comprehensible but the building of the chalk foundation upon which much of northern Europe rests is, to me, beyond comprehending. One, only one, microscopic single-celled creature built it with its frail, intricately sculpted shells, layer upon layer from the ocean floor. Upon it Ireland rests; and the south of England shored up by the White Cliffs of Dover; northern France and Germany and the Low Countries in between.

In the far past men supplied their crops with calcium without knowing it. They returned it to the soil when they spread the ash from their fires over the land. The Romans must have known that it was beneficial by the time they occupied the English Midlands. Fairly recent account has it that trails they made carrying limestone from the hills to their croplands can still be seen. But calcium, as calcium, was not known until 1808 after an English chemist invented a battery that gave him the electric arc which also led him to magnesium and potassium. Yet the fact that plants use calcium was not discovered until some 30 years later when scientists first analyzed plant ash for mineral content. This led to the further discovery that certain crops use more calcium than others.

The electric arc also disclosed the fact that these three alkalizers—calcium, magnesium and potassium—carry a positive electric charge. The full significance of this became apparent upon the discovery that clay and humus particles carry a negative electric charge. Consequently the negatively charged clay and humus attract and hold these positively charged elements against the downward pull of gravity. Nitrates and sulfates, however, are negatively charged and, since negative cannot attract and hold negative, these two elements slip through the soil quickly.

Nature plays a unique game of musical chairs based on this underground electrical attraction. Acidifying hydrogen, which is also positively charged, competes very successfully with the alkalizing minerals for a seat on the clay and humus particles. There is just so much room on a particle and when the hydrogen bumps off the alkalizers, the alkalizers dissolve in the soil water where some are absorbed and the rest wash away. The supply of hydrogen exceeds that of the minerals not only in wet areas but in average climates as well. For this reason the average soil tends more toward acidity than alkalinity.

When calcium's work is summed up we get the picture of an engineer who must oversee a number of important projects at the same time. Always dependable, always working in low profile, calcium strengthens cell walls as well as the entire skeletal structure while building the limbs of the young straight and unstunted. It works the clock around in leaves, roots and root hairs distributing carbohydrates and protein. In the soil it modifies acids produced by recyclers, vegetative growth, rain and other sources. Its positive electric charge separates negatively charged clay particles causing them to flock together in small groups, and this flocking leaves spaces for air and water flow.

As we all know, calcium is easily retrieved from home accumulations. Wood ashes carry such quantities of lime that they must be used sparingly. Bones, of course, add phosphorus to calcium and after a few hot fires disintegrate enough to speed up recycling. Farm women have long saved eggshells—I remember them drying in the warming oven of my mother's wood range and the dish was never empty. For so fragile a wrapper the shell of an egg breaks down very slowly and those I do not crush for the humus pile, mostly for aeration, I burn before putting into the soil.

Most calcium-carrying materials in garden shops come from ancient sea deposits or from crushed shells. Ground limestone rock and crushed shells provide calcium only, sometimes with small amounts of magnesium. Hydrated (slaked) lime has been steam treated and is quickly used. Dolomite carries both calcium and magnesium. Gypsum is sea-combined calcium and sulfur. It neither alkalizes nor acidifies the soil since the two elements neutralize one another. This combination makes gypsum of great value for supplying calcium to plants requiring acid soil.

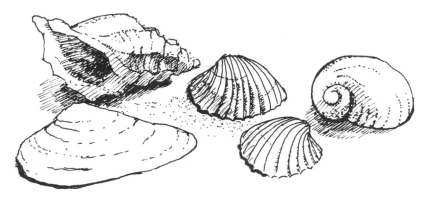

Dolomite (named for the French mineralogist, Dolomieu, not the Dolomite Alps) is very common and, like other minerals, has been making its epic journeys to the sea for ages lost in time. Niagara Falls is the scene of one of dolomite's most spectacular outward-bound trips. This great dolomitic ridge, over which the Falls plunge and which traces our eastern Canadian border, was built over long stretches of time by part of the Arctic sea bringing down and dropping great beds of the rock there. Once built, the Falls and the rivers have been scouring the mineral away, granule by granule, carrying it back to the sea where magnesium is second in quantity only to salt.

Plants use magnesium in making chlorophyll, oils and fats, and to help absorb and distribute phosphorus. Dolomite carries around 22% elemental calcium and 11% elemental magnesium which pleases the average plant in areas where rainfall is moderate to heavy. When spread on the humus pile the soil families multiply faster so finish their work sooner. And because bulky humus particles can hold more alkalizing elements than minute clay particles, these nutrients last longer in the soil when in the company of humus.

When using dolomite or wood ashes on the humus pile, two light coverings of about 1/8"–1/4" during its building is about right. The first application should be given when the pile has reached half its planned height, the last scattered over the top when finished, and each watered in gently.

When working alkalizing minerals directly into the soil everything is better served with a light application every year instead of a heavy one every 2–3 years. Lightly used, the soil maintains a steadier balance; the soil families are not thrown into a populating frenzy, quickly depleting the humus in the soil; and the plants have a stable flow of nutrients instead of a feast followed by famine. County agents recommend up to 5 pounds of dolomite or ground limestone per 100 square feet for established ornamentals in the average climate and soil. They recommend up to 10 pounds for 100 square feet of vegetables which seems overly much even where rainfall is above normal. Five pounds measure less than two quarts, and because the powder is so heavy more than intended can thud down.

There are two important points to remember when using alkalizing minerals. One is where to use them, the other is when to use them. More accurately, it is a matter of where and when *not* to use them. Never use them with nitrogenous fertilizers—urine, all manures, bottled organic fertilizers, or inorganic fertilizers containing nitrogen. The action of one upon the other generates carbon dioxide in the soil often in suffocating amounts killing or retarding plants and helpful soil families. Also, much of the nitrogen reverts to gas and escapes back to the atmosphere.

For this reason alkalizing materials should go into the soil at least two weeks before or after any nitrogen-carriers are used. With this in mind, spring is a good time to work dolomite, ground limestone, or ashes into the soil after it has drained sufficiently to be dug and aired. Mix the material into the upper inches and gently water it in. If left on top, the lime in dolomite and limestone forms a cement-like crust.

There are some precautions that I feel should be repeated to avoid disappointment. Among them is the warning to keep all alkalizing materials away from plants accustomed to the acid soil of high rainfall areas, woodlands, and swampy places. I list again some of the commonly grown: rhododendrons, azaleas, fuchsias, camellias, blueberries, blackberries, raspberries, evergreen trees and shrubs, ferns, oaks, chrysanthemums, heathers, magnolias, and most lilies. Also avoid all blue-flowering plants which often turn magenta or lavender or purple. Pinks and reds, outside the acid soil group, love a touch of it to intensify their color.

Plants accustomed to acid soil can get their calcium from gypsum, their magnesium from Epsom salts, and their sulfur from both. The sulfur in these compounds counteracts the alkalizing action of the calcium and magnesium. Sulfur is not only deeply involved in chlorophyll and protein production, but all plant functions deteriorate without it. In fact, it seems to be needed by everything that takes root, walks or flies. Birds need it for feathers, beaks and claws; animals for wool or whatever else they wear to protect themselves from the weather, and for hoof and horn. In us it promotes luxuriant hair and nails, and was considered a tonic to stir up winter-sluggish blood as children of the Edwardian era knew too well. Every spring they were backed into a corner and made to swallow sulfur and molasses.

We imported Sicilian sulfur mined from extinct volcanoes until we found the purest form of elemental sulfur in offshore beds in Louisiana and Texas. In the sea it combines with all major minerals except salt. It coalesced with the great chalk foundation that supports northern Europe and gypsum was the name given it being the Latin word for chalk. Technically it is calcium sulfate. An exceptionally soft, pure form of gypsum was found in the area where the city of Paris now stands and is the plaster of Paris from which surgical and ornamental casts are made. French farmers used to fertilize their land with a mixture of gypsum, charcoal and dried night soil which they called poudrette. In my childhood the farmers called gypsum land plaster, and those who used it every spring on their strawberries found that their crop was heavier and ripened earlier than others.

As time goes on I become more and more enamored of gypsum. It can be used as nutrient and soil conditioner anywhere in the garden with the happy assurance that everything that happens, happens for the best. After a winter of excess rain when even good soil packs, it can work a spring miracle in a short time. When used in the fall, its flocking action reduces winter packing. I first started using gypsum in powder form and measure it as I do dolomite keeping it to around 5 pounds for 100 square feet. Now that it is being granulated I simply scatter it like a light fall of hail, turn it in lightly and water. Gypsum, to me, is a wonder-working combination of minerals.

Epsom salts (magnesium sulfate) is really richer in light background material than garden support. Once the most commonly used purgative, it is not without romance. It takes its name from the famous spa at Epsom to which fashionable 18th and 19th century Londoners coached every May. The short journey took them through the countryside at a time when the cowslips were beginning to nod in the meadows and pastures, and the nightingales' last notes still quavered in the copses. At first the annual visit was made solely to take the mineral waters for a serving out after a winter of rich and heavy meals. But this polite purpose left the twelfth Earl of Derby with enough time on his hands to inject some life into the dedicated outing by instituting the first Derby there in 1780, winning with his three-year-old Diomed.

But to return to Epsom salts for garden use. It is not the all-around treasure gypsum is, yet it can do amazing things for acid soil plants wanting a magnesium lift, and the little that is needed costs practically nothing. The $1 box from the garden shop will last all my rhododendrons indefinitely since I have used it only once in my time here. But that once keeps recycling year after year in the fallen leaves and blooms. I used 2 scant tablespoons in the 9 quart watering can, first dissolving the crystals in a pint of hot water before adding the cold. Since rhododendrons are shallow rooting, the one thorough soak from trunk to branch tips will satisfy them for many years.

The trial was made on a 60 foot base planting featuring a low-branching variety which I treated in early summer after spring bloom. The following April and May the large, lustrous pink-red bells jostled one another around for position all but hiding the new leaves of freshly polished brass. It has been so every year since. However, the planting is below the bay windows and growth has now become a problem though no other fertilizer has been used except the recyclers'.

There are times when soil needs sulfur to acidify it—when it has been overloaded with alkalizing materials, where waste mortar has accumulated, when plants requiring acid soil are grown outside rainy areas, or in gardens where average rainfall is low. Peat moss, oak leaf or evergreen needle mold acidify to some extent but for an acute condition sulfur is needed. Our county agent recommends ½ cup per square yard worked in lightly and very lightly watered since it is quick to leave the soil.

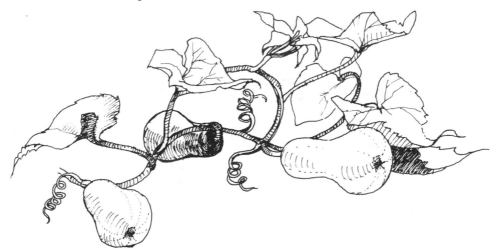

Trace Elements (micronutrients)

There are 7 trace elements which, as the name implies, are needed only in trace amounts. If we return to the soil the waste material from our own garden, and all the peels, cores, leaves, husks, rinds and roots of the fruits and vegetables we buy, no more will be needed. Agriculture must use micronutrients in the constant turnover of crops. What is taken from the soil is passed on, in organic form, with enough left in the waste for recycling over and over again in our gardens.

Trace elements are like the tiny jewels in fine old watches and often no more than one part per million is needed to make the agricultural watch run smoothly. They function mainly as catalysts to activate the primary and secondary feeding elements. Certain ones for certain needs—to prevent celery from cracking, apples from "corking", root crops from "brown heart" and splitting. What was used by the agriculturist's current crop leaves with that crop and a compensating amount must be replaced for the next.

Of these seven micronutrients—iron, boron, copper, manganese, molybdenum, zinc, and chlorine—only iron will be mentioned because of the popular involvement with iron chelates. Liebig found iron in plant ash but the other six remained unknown until this century. About 30–40 years ago, iron was combined with certain organic compounds to sequester, or hold, the element in available form. They called this product chelated iron and it was first formulated for agriculturists working low rainfall areas where alkaline minerals lock iron into unavailability.

Chelated iron benefits only the gardener in dry regions, or the one who has over-alkalized his average or acid soil, or who is growing acid soil plants against cement foundations. There can be no dearth of iron in the soil, only alkaline lock-up. Of the nutrient elements in the earth's crust, iron leads with 5.1% followed by calcium's 3.6%, but the two have been in conflict since the planet was in the making. Every cataclysmic convulsion catapulted iron up from the depths of the earth. And with every such upheaval the sea retreated leaving behind the great calcium-carrying foundations. But no one seems to know why the calcified remains of sea life throws the mineral metal of the earth's core into a state of impotency.

The packets of iron chelates offered in the garden shops here carry the recommendation that it be used on plants with yellowing leaves. Of course we know this should be taken seriously only when previously mentioned conditions responsible for yellowing leaves have been corrected or do not exist. Adding iron to soil that is poorly drained, or suffering for water, or lacking nitrogen or sulfur, or for any other mismanagement that causes leaves to yellow will do no harm, but neither will it do any good.

In these fertilizer facts can be caught a glimpse of the prolonged, convulsive labor this planet endured to bring forth life; and something of how it conserves its vital resources to last, as they must, if life is to last. We cannot possibly grasp the awesomeness of the world's genesis but, even so, we should never take it for granted. The wonder of it is there in every soft flower. Wordsworth spoke of this when he said of Peter Bell—

> A primrose by a river's brim,
> A yellow primrose was to him,
> And it was nothing more.

7
Air Power

I have three friends, all renowned gardeners, whose ages average 94. In their knarled trunks the sap still rises every spring, and in their eyes humor plays with wisdom the year around. While cutting roses one asked if I had ever noticed how some of their fragrance always seems to cling to the hand that gives them. She regretted that so few of us take time any more to smell our flowers, that we are letting this pleasure, like the giving of them, slip away from us. These three women still cultivate their gardens and all agree that the simple act of cultivation brings health to plants and cultivator alike and, with it, a restorative union with the earth.

Most of the time I cultivate my garden more for its welfare than mine. But there are times when I cultivate it for mine alone. I am drawn to the soil by my need of it much as a child is drawn to its mother. When I sit in her brown lap, my hands working her body as childrens' hands do, she quiets me. So to me and my three old friends who have for so long been taking our griefs and joys to the soil for bearing, today's emphasis on token gardening leaves spirit, body, and plant denied.

Advertisements encourage us to beautify our grounds because it is the thing to do. They offer garden cosmetics for the beautiful look suggesting that there is not time for much else in today's tight and stressful schedules. Yet medical men now prescribe physical action to counterbalance stress just as philosophers of old taught the healing power of simple activities. In the last 30–40 years stress has surfaced as a direct cause of serious illness and one of the treatments many doctors prescribe for themselves and others is gardening.

I have seen the lion of the office become a lamb in his garden as he looks with satisfaction on the work of his hands and muscles. He has mingled his sweat with the sweat of the soil warming in the spring sun. He has felt the sensuous touch of the summer breeze running light fingers over his body. When he and autumn prepare for the winter, he enjoys again the spring and summer past and plans for the spring and summer to come. His garden is a quiet place in the eye of the storm. In it, tensions and damaging emotions drop away. And as peace of mind gains momentum it activates his physical defenses which, in turn, bring up reinforcements.

His blood courses with renewed vigor stimulated by the exercise and purified by deep draughts of oxygen. When we lived more naturally we got our oxygen in the course of our daily rounds. Now many of us realize that our breathing habits need looking into, and when the cultivating gardener looks into his he is also looking after the oxygen needs of those living in his soil. Everything breathes after its own fashion. We have the advantage of lungs and blood to conduct oxygen to cells and tissues but plants and soil families must absorb oxygen where it is needed.

Jethro Tull was the first to think of leaves as lungs and though this is not exactly true it certainly was advanced thinking in the 18th century. Even in the early 19th, when Liebig was a student, chemistry was still a philosophy and questions were considered vulgar. Universities and colleges gave no credits for chemistry which often amounted to a few lectures some country clergyman gave once a year. Liebig, at Giessen, was the first professor of chemistry to allow students to participate in laboratory and field experiments so, until that time, it was the self-trained investigator who made the first advances in plant behavior. One was a Swiss scientist and naturalist who, working at home around the year 1800, proved that plants respire.

Should plants ever fail to respire we would suffocate before we starved. There is just so much oxygen in the atmosphere, and if plants did not recycle it for reuse from our breathing waste (carbon dioxide), the supply would shortly end. The margin between supply and demand is estimated at about 1%—the atmosphere contains 21% oxygen and, of this, about 20% is considered necessary to sustain life. In this colossal recycling plan Nature achieves her most supreme economy while performing a sleight of hand trick. Green life absorbs the exhaled waste of all red-blooded life and from this, and combustion waste, makes 90% of its food. And while the food is in the making, oxygen is being released back into the atmosphere for reuse.

To the plant, this is an everyday occurrence. Since the first greening, life above and below ground has been juggling the earth's oxygen, nitrogen, hydrogen and carbon. The nitrogen that we inhale with oxygen we return to the atmosphere unchanged. The oxygen we change to carbon dioxide. The plants' leaves absorb our waste product during the daytime, but only in the daytime because the sun is needed to power this miracle we call photosynthesis. While the leaves are absorbing carbon dioxide they are also splitting water—taken up by the roots—into hydrogen and oxygen. The oxygen they release back into the atmosphere. The hydrogen they keep and combine it with the carbon dioxide to produce glucose upon which, in one way or another, all life depends.

Our life, and the way we live it, and all our energy-related wealth, hang upon a leaf's greenness. It is the chlorophyll in the leaf that traps the sun's radiant energy needed to power the sugar-making machinery. It is the chlorophyll, with sun energy, that combines the inorganic gases and converts them to organic sugar in a split second. With light and warmth plants make their sugar, or glucose (sometimes called dextrose, grape or corn sugar) faster than they can use it. What they cannot immediately use they store in their leaves as starch until night when they change much of it back to sugar and distribute it to all their parts.

When the sun quits work for the day, leaf respiration reverses. The leaves then take in oxygen and give off carbon dioxide as we and all animals do. The sugar-making factory automatically shuts down for the night which gives the plant time to distribute the day's excess food and do its fastest growing. But as soon as the sun is up, the leaves go back to absorbing carbon dioxide, releasing oxygen, and making sugar. Land plants make some 40 billion tons of glucose a year, sea plants some 260 billion tons. If scientists ever succeed in harnessing solar power with chlorophyll, plants will be supplying us with energy as well as food and oxygen. But as yet no man-made device has been able to duplicate the sun-powered converters in the green leaves of a plant. The communication between sun and leaf remains a planetary mystery.

Since roots take in oxygen and expel carbon dioxide day and night, a porous soil is their only means of intake and outgo. Nature has no difficulty keeping her soil porous. She never misses an autumn to pile more leaves on the duff of the forest floor, or to fold over the meadows the grass and leaves and flowers that served their purpose in the spring and summer. Her children walk and scratch and burrow with light feet bringing air. Our feet block out air every time we walk on the soil when it is wet. And we deny our soil its rightful air-filtering residues every time we are wastefully neat.

Leaves mirror the good health or illness of the roots as surely as the sea mirrors the sky. The old adage "mischief shows in the leaves but lies at the root" is as true today as when it was minted 100 years ago. And the chief mischief-maker is still the lack of oxygen. Roots are wonderfully made, little marvels in themselves. Each tapered tip wears a cap of cells which is constantly breaking down and renewing to produce a slippery film. This film lubricates the root for an easier and deeper penetration of the soil and when the soil is spongy and open the thrust is deep enough to satisfy plant needs.

Life can exist for some time without food, less without water, but no time at all without oxygen. The gardener's first consideration for his soil and the life it supports should be air and water circulation. Cultivation and

humus and water when needed is such a simple health program that it is apt to pass us by. Somewhere along the line we began to believe that a thing was good only if we bought it. Yet it is always where these natural needs have been denied the roots that leaves turn yellow, spot or drop before it is their time to decay and fall.

A fertile soil is often half open space and half solid particles. These open spaces, or pores, are filled partly with water and partly with air. A beautifully engineered pumping system keeps the two circulating. As water moves into the pores it forces out the roots' waste carbon dioxide. And as the water drains from the pores, oxygen flows in. I have already said, probably too many times, that early spring is an especially hard time for plants. But let me say this just once more—give them humus and a good cultivation to send fresh air to their roots, then watch them undulate with the rhythm of life like oriental dancers, feet never moving.

Even so, I know that some of the leaves of some of these plants will yellow or spot and quietly slough away, or drop, a few months after cultivation. We take no alarm when we see leaves publicly preparing for their autumnal fall but often do when we see old leaves privately preparing to die in the summer. We should learn the difference between ill health and the normal leaf decay of spring blooming perennials and roses after the plants bloom. The mission of these leaves ended with the flowering. Old leaves must die to make room for the new and the building of the next flower crop. Always it is a normal function if new leaves appear while the old are dying, or shortly after they drop or disappear. We know then that all is well and another feeding cycle has begun.

In soils well aired with humus there is an amazing activity going on that is highly beneficial to plant health. It is the production of antibiotics. The soil is home to many microscopic families other than the housekeepers, recyclers and converters. Most are benign and some of them produce certain antibiotic substances. These families increase with the increasing humus and dwindle as it decreases. But the malign families can, if need be, flourish in deteriorating or impoverished soil bringing disease with their increasing numbers. When the two engage in the age-old struggle for food and living space, antibiotic production begins. As soon as the disease-producers start invading benign territory, each antibiotic-producing family encircles its colony with its own kind of protective substance barricading itself against the invaders. These antibiotics curb infections in plant life as they do in ours.

After penicillin came to light in the 1940s, microbiologists found that other soil families were producing hormones and vitamins as well as the so-called miracle drugs—among them vitamin B_{12} which has controlled anemia. Some of these families are bacteria, some are molds, some are half one and half the other, each with a unique beauty of color and form. Laboratories now grow them in astronomical numbers and induce them to produce their specialties in commercial quantities.

Unlike benign families, the disease-producers can live in poorly drained, packed soil carrying as little as 2% oxygen. Plants cannot live where soil oxygen is less than 50% and, because helpful soil families are primarily plant-like in their requirements, it is reasonable to assume that they, too, must have a minimum of 50% oxygen to live.

Since Tull's time we have become aware of the influence that cultivation, air and humus have on one another and on the soil. Tull first saw plowing between rows practiced in the vineyards of southern France and took the idea back home with him. Since his drill sowed seed in rows, he tried tilling corn and other row crops with his cultivators and found between-the-row tillage as beneficial to food and fodder plants as to grapes.

After thoroughly testing his new system he published a book in 1733 explaining and defending it. Its title must be shared: *Horse-hoeing Husbandry; or, An Essay on the Principles of Tillage and Vegetation, wherein is taught a Method of introducing a sort of Vinyard Culture into the Corn-Fields, in order to increase their Product and diminish the Common Expense.* It is unbelievable that only a few among the literate accepted the system as an advance. The rest called him everything from an ass and an atheist to a madman and carping insect. The illiterate viewed the whole thing with suspicion and alarm.

Exactly 200 years separate Tull's horse-hoeing husbandry and our Dust Bowl disaster. One put cultivation in motion, the other carried it to excess. At the turn of this century, dust-mulching as a means of conserving moisture became popular with dry-land farmers. The purpose was to keep a layer of loose soil over the surface which would act as a lid on evaporation by checking the upward capillary movement of water. But as time went on the disadvantages inherent in dust-mulching became obvious.

Cultivating after a rain to conserve moisture extended to cultivating in times of drought in the hope of conserving what little moisture remained. Unfortunately, what little organic matter remained was recycled all the more quickly leaving the lifeless soil particles completely free to blow away on the wind. In such circumstances every cultivation was a disaster. Clods would have been better than dust, and drought-resistant grass better than clods.

Before dust-mulching was generally abandoned its popularity spread to farmers and home gardeners working average soil. But if they cultivated the soil before it had dried enough to avoid packing they did more harm than a questionable good. And if they waited until the soil was dry enough to work, much of the water had already evaporated which automatically capped

the surface with a dry layer. Certainly the use of organic matter to structure the soil made dust-mulching obsolete. The home garden needs but one deep cultivation in the spring to drain and air it. Light cultivation in the summer could be looked upon as a way to fertilize the soil since air speeds up the recyclers' work.

Everyone who cultivates has probably settled upon a favorite tool so I feel free to give my reasons for favoring the tines over the broad blades. For spring work the digging fork is indispensable. It is my plow, smasher, harrow, leveler, smoother, and perforator, depending upon how I handle it. Forking down straight and deep for new beds and vegetable plantings meets with no resistance compared to the combative bite of a shovel or spade. On the borders I do a deeper, more efficient job with less energy by pushing the fork with my foot instead of thrusting a trowel with my arm. On my knees, with tines horizontal, I reach under the rhododendrons and perforate and loosen the soil. This gives them a light root pruning which, contrary to warnings against cutting roots, stimulates growth and bloom.

Nurserymen know that root pruning produces stronger, bushier root systems and therefore tops. At Barnhaven I learned that certain plants refuse to set seed in the cultivated state unless their roots are cut. Strawberry growers may still root prune to increase the yield. The only explanation I can think of—certainly totally unscientific—is that the plant feels itself threatened. It must produce more seeds to guarantee survival so more flowering must be done. It must grow more roots for a greater intake of food and water and to repair the minor breaks in its foothold. Actually, from the end of every cleanly cut or broken root many new rootlets grow.

I do not deliberately root prune rhododendrons, roses and other perennials. But if spring cultivation is to achieve its purpose of opening the soil for air and water circulation to reach the entire rooting area, then a few roots are going to be cut. When nurserymen root prune they wait until rain is expected or gently irrigate immediately after to bring cut ends and soil into close contact again. When I deeply cultivate, the spring soil is pleasantly moist. Still, if there is no darkening of the sky seaward, I water very softly to reunite the roots with the soil.

The digging fork is a gentle tool and can go where the relentless, solid-cutting blades of shovel and spade cannot. It is an agile, graceful tool easy on the handler. But there are times when the trowel is needed for things other than planting and the narrow, in my estimation, is preferable to the wide. A hand fork is necessary for cultivating plants with creeping root-stocks and I really like it better for general light work than the trowel. For shallow summer cultivation the quick and dexterous, long-handled miniature rake (about 3½'' wide with four 2½'' tines on a 4' handle) is a positive delight. It scratches around the necks of plants and reaches far back into the spaces between, uprooting young weeds to dry in the sun. But for cultivating in tight garden spots, potted plants, and seedlings, the only tools for the job are the ice pick and the carving fork.

The hardest thing to learn about cultivating one's garden is when to quit. The satisfaction of seeing the soil crumble under the tool, the exhilaration of renewing and being renewed, can lead us beyond a pleasing tiredness. This is no problem for me on windy days, or when everything around me is a dampish pussywillow gray. But on still days, when the sun is a topaz set in blue enamel, and the earth is warm and I am warm, quitting is not easy. Yet I learned a good while ago that fatigue does not erase the satisfaction or the exhilaration for long. My three old friends know it. My mother knew it. And my great-grandmother who had a habit of saying after a long, hard day in the fields, "Ah, work makes the rest so sweet". And so it does.

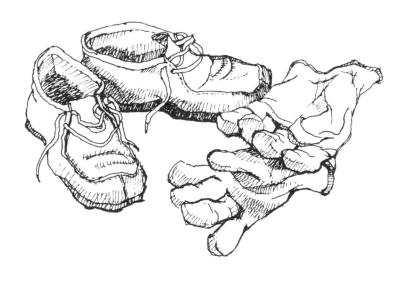

8
Mulches and Moles

THE MEADOW

There is a highway running west through the farmlands of the valley that crosses the coastal mountains and turns south here to follow the sea to San Francisco. A stone's throw from the bend in the road is a meadow. It drops a hundred feet and more sheer to the sea. Often I stand there on its flowered edge looking down at the waves being turned over by an unseen plow, then out to where the distance has smoothed the furrows into a flat and fertile field.

This is an enchanted meadow. My years slip away into another's lifetime as I pick the same flowers I picked as a child in the Valley and feel the same guilt when they melt in my hand. Reality is no more than a wisp of drifting fog. How can it be that this abandoned Indian land, this 40-acre island of tranquillity still lies quiet and untouched on the edge of traffic never ending, never stopping unless to shop before hurtling on. How is it that I never meet another walking through the low drifts of pink and lavender and plum colored wild iris in the spring? Or see no one kneeling to smell the fragrant purple violets that shelter in the lee of the wild roses? That there are no tracks but mine among the azure camas lilies edging the little stream whose water is cold and sweet in the mouth?

In early summer I pick the wild strawberries. In late summer, huckleberries and the little blackberries whose hidden vines trip me when I walk carelessly. When my hands are not full I sack up some of the mole hills, unable to resist the rich black earth. In the fall I watch how the grasses and the columbines and Queen Anne's Lace fold themselves over themselves so lightly, and over the low growing plants finished now with their flowering and fruiting. Once again the meadow has mulched itself.

We mulch our gardens in different ways but for the same reasons. We protect our plants with some light and airy material in the cold months as needed and remove the cover when need is over. Only Nature has the knack of removing her winter cover by settling it around the plants in the spring, letting it sink back into the earth to feed and protect in the summer. We duplicate this action when we cover the soil with organic material in the warming months, feeding and comforting our plants and underground families when they are working at top speed. To do this we must have on hand sufficient humus or know where we can get enough raw material to make up the difference.

Our shrubs and trees and perennials will help mulch themselves with their fallen leaves and petals if we let them. Yet even with their help, and all the other garden waste and kitchen waste, the humus pile can run short if called upon to cover an extensive area. If it does, there are two sources of raw organic material, both free. In the fall we can gather the rich autumn leaves and add their nutrients and bulk to the pile ripening over the winter. And valuable discards from the produce markets can usually be had for the collecting.

If we choose to save a step by putting the raw material directly on the soil we are following Ruth Stout's System which she started some 40 years ago in Connecticut to save time, labor and water while building her soil and raising exceptional crops. She found that by keeping the soil deeply mulched the year around almost all work in her flower and vegetable plots, except planting, thinning and picking, was eliminated. The method does away with weeding and cultivating, water is seldom needed, and there is no soil preparation other than covering it with kitchen and garden waste and hay.

Hay is all-important to the Stout System. This means locating a source of supply and a place to store it which may be easy for rural and town gardeners but not for others. If hay is available, try to find spoiled bales. They are comparatively cheap, and though the hay is unfit for feeding cattle because of rain damage its worth as a feeding mulch is in no way impaired. Alfalfa hay is a particularly good buy with an analysis of 2½% nitrogen, ½% phosphorus, and 2% potash. The nutrient value of alfalfa straw is cut almost in half. Still the amount of nitrogen and potash in the straw is more than twice that in horse and cow manure.

The Stout System encourages gardening among those whose time or strength is at a minimum, and those who do not enjoy working the soil as much as others. It is easily followed. Begin by covering the soil, sod and all, with hay to a depth of 8" to kill the weeds. Very shortly this fluffy cover settles down to about 2–3". As the housekeepers recycle the hay to humus, weeds will appear through the thinning mulch. These and any bare spots should then be covered with more hay, kitchen and garden waste, or any other soft organic material available. Always the soil and weeds must be kept covered.

Seeds are planted only when the soil beneath the mulch has mellowed. Start by pushing back the mulch (which is again about 2–3" deep) from either side of the proposed row to make a bare strip for sowing. After that, the seeding procedure goes on as usual. Make a shallow trench down the middle of the exposed strip, sow the seeds, cover very lightly with soil, tamp down, and gently water in. Then pull the mulch back up to the planted row, never covering it, just as you pull the covers up to the chin of a child.

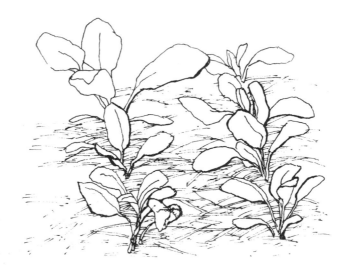

In midwinter, or when cold weather sets in, cottonseed meal or soybean meal is scattered over the mulch (5# to 100 square feet) for the rains and melting snow to wash into the soil. I do not know the analysis of soybean meal but the cottonseed meal offered here is all nitrogen, 6% which is high. With the hay and waste running to nitrogen, and the cloistered nitrogen fixers converting atmospheric nitrogen in the pea and bean patch, and the lazy nitrogen fixers working now and then in the undisturbed soil, there is no lack of feeding nitrates.

Should I adopt the Stout System in its entirety I would substitute steamed bone meal for the nitrogenous meals. The high percentage of phosphorus in bone meal would compensate for the low percentage in vegetable waste and hay, relieve the soil's general phosphorus deficiency, and satisfy the plants' great need of it. But several things keep me from year-round mulching. I am not in hay country nor have I space to store it were it available. And I love working the soil, love seeing it grow black and rich under my hands. The more obvious kitchen waste that I barely turn under in the borders quickly becomes part of the soil. And the pods, tops and old flowers laid on top of the soil are worn with the dignity of common sense. What covers and protects its body in summer becomes part of it by spring.

I know nothing about the mulching products offered for sale outside my region. We do not have buckwheat hulls, or cocoa bean hulls, or bagasse (crushed sugar-cane or sugar-beet refuse) but I think of them, wrongly perhaps, as being more cosmetic than nutritious. What we do have in quantity is peat from the bogs of British Columbia, and wood waste from California's redwoods, and from the firs and other softwoods of the Pacific Northwest. So it is peat and wood products that we know and use more often, sometimes with unfortunate results.

The large, empty leaf cells of peat moss absorb and store significant amounts of water which makes peat of value in dry soils, and in seeding and potting mixtures. In my opinion, this is its one and only reliable attribute. As a mulch, peat moss can dry into a brittle sheet when needed most. Should this occur, it soaks up whatever moisture comes its way since the leaf cells are not satisfied with just a moistening. They are reservoirs, taking and holding as much water as possible from overhead sources and sponging it up from the soil. Consequently, under certain circumstances, a peat mulch can rob the soil of moisture from above and below instead of conserving it.

There are some 300 species of peat, or bog, mosses. All are members

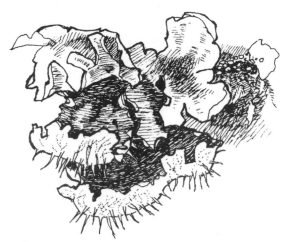

of the sphagnum family and not one of them can be counted on for much of anything except holding moisture in the soil and in propagating mixtures. Nutrients are practically nonexistent which doubtless accounts for its remaining unrecycled for years. When peat moss finally is recycled, little or no humus remains. Because mosses grow only in exceedingly wet places, peat is naturally acid and therefore better used around plants liking the acid conditions of wetter than average soil. But to work water-holding peat into such soil, unless it is thin and in need of binding, is carrying coals to Newcastle.

Wood products, particularly barkdust, can also rob the soil of moisture from above and below. When the lumber industry began grinding its mountains of accumulated bark and promoting it for garden use, they turned a big problem into a big profit. Nurserymen hoped to do the same by using it. It promised to eliminate cultivation and to conserve moisture, and so reduce labor and water bills. Rhododendron growers were especially enthused since their stock is surface rooting and needs moist soil at ground level as well as below.

I still remember the experience of one of the first to use barkdust in my area. His nursery was not far from Barnhaven where rainfall can be relied upon in all seasons except summer. He planned to hold the moisture of the wet months throughout the dry months until the rains began again in the fall. After fielding out his young rhododendrons in the spring and mulching with about 3″ of barkdust, he turned on the irrigation system for three days and nights to thoroughly settle in the plants and saturate the mulch. By midsummer, leaves began to yellow and drop. When the county agent was called in to diagnose the disease he simply raked away the mulch and exposed bone-dry soil. The plants were dying for lack of water.

Home gardeners who use barkdust should realize that it can keep the soil dry in summer even though they water. More often the gardener does not water thinking that the mulch is holding enough moisture in the soil. So when leaves yellow or drop the plants are either treated for an imagined disease or given a fast-acting nitrogenous fertilizer. We know of course this can do no good, that it is like dosing or force-feeding a person or animal struggling for air or dying of thirst.

Gardeners who like the sun tanned look are better off with a light scattering of bark chips which can admit water. Other than this I see no difference between the chunky product and the finely ground. Both take but cannot give in the raw state. But when wood is eventually recycled to humus, there is nothing better. British Columbians used to make trips into their mountains to sack up rotted stumps and logs. They were unusually quiet about it but the secret leaked, as gardening secrets will, which sent us into our mountains for the magical stuff. Roots love to thread their way through the dark brown sponge smelling of deep woods and ferns and damp earth, absorbing the nutrients that once supported a tree.

Rotted sawdust approximates the decayed remains of trees but, for me, cannot duplicate it—though it may be the intangible experience of the forest that cannot be duplicated. However, rotted sawdust can seldom be found any more, even the raw is increasingly hard to locate. A great amount of energy is required to recycle raw wood products to humus and unless nitrogen is added the recyclers will take it from the soil. It is a sad sight to see plants struggling to grow where raw sawdust has been worked into the soil without supplementing nitrogen. They sit there stunted, yellow and starved, because the recyclers need and take all the available nitrate to complete their arduous work. Perhaps the best way to use sawdust—as a mulch as well as in the soil—is to first pile it about 2′ deep in more shade than sun like a humus heap, wet it down well, add nitrogen in a quickly available form, and keep it moist until it becomes brown and porous. More than one application of nitrogen will be needed.

If the soil is mulched in the fall to protect plant roots over the winter, the material should be one that cannot leach nitrogen, particularly around winter-active plants. Had I used hay instead of dairy manure between the nursery rows of primroses that disastrous fall, loss could have been reduced. There would have been no urine to stimulate growth during the long Indian summer and the hay could easily have been pulled over the plants when the freeze struck. The top growth would have had some protection in the absence of snow. Snow is the perfect winter cover and how we rejoice when it falls. Hardy evergreen perennials that winterkill here in a snowless freeze with its wind and sun, winter safely under the snows of our northern and northeastern states in much lower temperatures. And plants used to wintering there can winterkill here in a milder climate that is subject to abrupt drops without snow coverage.

The material used for winter covering, or in winter emergencies, must be light and airy, something that will not pack. Though the reason for covering evergreen plants in a snowless freeze is more to shield their leaves from the wind and sun than for warmth, the temperature will be slightly raised. A 19th century Englishman made an experiment to determine the degree of rise by placing a handkerchief over four stakes elevated 6″ above his lawn. He claimed that the temperature under the handkerchief rose 8° F above that of the surrounding exposed area. Sometime I will check it.

Evergreen boughs are one of the most satisfactory coverings. They are quickly put on, protect yet admit air, do not blow off, are quickly removed when the weather moderates, easily stacked against the next emergency, and as easily reduced to ash in the spring. Fir boughs are ideal but a good canopy cover can be made from prunings of evergreens and miscellaneous light limbs saved during the year, perhaps augmented by neighborly contributions. If it can be found, wood excelsior gives excellent, airy protection and quickly sacks up like new material for reuse year after year. Whatever the covering, it should be on hand before November.

In predictable climates, where frosts are usually on schedule followed by freeze and snow, hay seems to be the favored covering. If it is mulchers' hay it can be used in the spring as a soil cover after it comes off the plants. Fallen leaves, because they become sodden and mat, are not a safe plant cover in unpredictable climates. The object of overhead protection is to shield foliage and crowns yet allow adequate air circulation to prevent rotting or smothering; and to prevent or reduce root breakage when the soil heaves during freeze and thaw. Plants that have been set out too late to root deeply before freezing weather begins will be in dire need of overhead protection in vacillating climates.

The weather always has the last word in a garden, a word that becomes an order when winter protection is to go on and when it is to come off. The covering should go on after the soil freezes and left on until it thaws. Where the climate is flighty, hardy evergreen plants will weather a short period of snowless freeze that does not drop much below 25° F. The plants will replace any leaves that have been burned by sun and wind in the next growing period, but these will be very tender and must have protection in the next light freeze. However, when a 25° F, or lower, snowless freeze lasts longer than 3 or 4 days, it certainly is advisable to cover evergreen plants. In variable climates, hardy herbaceous plants need no protection. Where the climate is cold enough to warrant protecting the entire garden, hay is put on gradually in thin layers beginning after the first few frosts, finishing by the time the temperature has dropped to around 25° F. It is also removed gradually over a period of 2 or 3 weeks to harden new growth, and is altogether off by the time the grass begins to green.

Then, once again, it is the renewal—immortal spring with its mysterious stirrings, throbbing through everything that lives. All green-blooded and red-blooded life quickens in unison with the growing warmth, and in much the same way. Even the one-celled families in the soil, and the earthworms—who thinks about the earthworm's response to spring, or that he has one. We know that he is the gardener's friend and the barometer of our soil's health, but we do not know that everything about him and his way of life is astonishing, even touching. Very little has been written about him as a being, living in a society of his own.

He is a wonder of design. His 5 pairs of aortic loops encircle his esophagus to circulate blood. He has a rudimentary brain and a keen sensory system in place of sight and hearing. His simple digestive tract is like a bird's with a gizzard and a crop to digest and an unimpeded channel for elimination. And like a bird, he does not foul his nest but works his way to the surface and there casts his wastes. He propels himself by contracting and relaxing his dual muscular system, and by gripping the walls of the burrow with his 4 pairs of bristles and pushing. On the return trip he brings back organic matter if he remains whole. But if a robin catches him, and his bristled hooks slacken under the pulling and part of him is lost, he must return empty-handed and grow new parts.

Earthworms live in moist soils containing humus which is their food and shelter. They work when it is warm and sleep when it is cold but if they are forced to spend a freezing winter in exposed thin soil, some will die and others will leave in search of a protected sleeping place. In such places as the stream banks of my meadow, they leave their shallow horizontal corridors when the earth grows too cold for everyday living and make tunnels among the roots of the pines and spruce. The passages join to form sleeping galleries and there, relatively safe from moles, they sleep twined around one another in comforting communes. The 5 pairs of aortic loops now circulate only enough blood to maintain life.

When the cosmic force of spring brushes each one with a feather's touch, all 10 of his incipient hearts quicken. He untangles himself from the others and starts swallowing earth for the organic matter it contains. With the coming of spring a new generation has increased his numbers for only the most mature among the elders failed to survive. Young and old build topsoil with their castings, and mix humus and raw organic matter with the subsoil when they return. Their tunnelings cultivate and open the soil for greater air and water circulation and provide channels for roots to grow into. They bind soil particles together by coating them with their adhesive secretions. And those who died supplied as much as 40# of nitrate to the acre from the protein they stored in their bodies to see them through their winter sleep.

When I return my household and garden waste to the soil I try to remember to mix gratitude with it for the earthworms since this is all I can give them in return for the vast amount of good they do. The surest way to judge the condition of our soil is to take note of their numbers. If we see them often we know that the humus content is sufficient for all the life it supports. If we seldom see them we know that there is no point in buying them because they will not stay where organic matter is too scant to feed and shelter them.

If there are gardens where the soil is rich in humus and earthworms but free of moles, I have yet to hear about them. Earthworms are the moles' bread and butter and as the worm population increases, the moles increase. When I had barely half a dozen anemic earthworms I had no moles, but as soon as the worm families multiplied the runs and hills began to appear. At Barnhaven I trapped moles successfully but regretfully feeling a sadness in the killing. It seemed that each one had strayed from the pages of *The Wind in the Willows* intending no harm as he went about his daily affairs. Now I no longer have to kill to keep them out of my garden. Quite by accident I found that I could exploit their sensory system to warn them of danger though it existed only on the waves of their supersensitive perception.

On the last day of trapping here I stood holding a limp body, hating myself as I ran a finger over his glossy black velvet coat and down the bare digging hands so shapely and white. The five slender fingers, tapered with fashionably long nails, were the fingers of a model with a miner's strength. Before I could properly bury him I was called away and hurriedly stuffed the

body into the run and closed it. This was a main thoroughfare coming in from under the street and I just happened to head him back the way he came in. Several months went by before I realized that no moles had returned. I reasoned that the decaying body was sending danger signals through the run and that none would return until all odor and traces of death had disappeared.

I assumed that any meat would have the same effect after it began to decay. On hand was a pound of liver—a painless sacrifice—and down the middle of the west lawn was a Maginot line of hills. I pushed aside each mound of soil and troweled open the run beneath. With kitchen tongs I pushed a slice of liver as far as possible into the opened runway, both directions. I then rammed several handfuls of the loose soil hard against both openings, pounding it tight with my fist to keep the fumes concentrated in each section of the run. After that it was only a matter of putting back the loose soil and turf and hosing it back in place.

Just once has the system failed me and, then, for only a short time. When the moles kept coming in last winter, having been absent during the warm months, I realized that the cold soil refrigerated the meat and prevented its rotting. I then let the meat ripen indoors before putting it in the runs and the system again was activated. I often do this even in warm weather and feel repaid for the minute or two of unpleasantness since it is immediately effective.

Very shortly I realized that buying meat was unnecessary. Meat and poultry trimmings do just as well and commit the entire kitchen waste to the soil. Since two or three months go by before the runs need stuffing again, I freeze the scraps as they accumulate and use them as needed. So the only cost of enclosing my garden within this magic circle is a little time now and then. Vegetation booms where roots can syphon off the residues. I am reminded of the Indian practice of planting a fish under each hill of corn they sowed. No odor escapes in the garden to attract dogs and cats if the run openings are tightly plugged with soil, the troweled-out area solidly refilled, and stamped down until level with the surface, then watered.

Hair combings used in the same way are equally effective. Who knows whether it is the human odor that frightens or fear of entangling hands and feet. I have used hair in the runs, bunched or loosely coiled around the finger, and found it to be a long-lasting deterrent. Moles are now a rarity in this earthworm Utopia.

The other morning while walking in the meadow I stopped to watch the way the grass was trembling under the wind's light touch and saw a mole scrambling about here and there for some reason known only to himself. He was full-grown, sleek and fat and it was hard to believe that he had lost his way. Perhaps I wanted to believe that this was the same kind of morning that made Mole in *The Wind in the Willows* come out to play. To come out and roll and dance in the sun and forget about whitewashing the walls around his fireplace, and getting on with the rest of his spring housecleaning. For a moment it was easy to believe because this is an enchanted meadow too.

9
Planting Principles and Plant Hunters

VIOLETS IN THE FLAGSTONES

Washington State University's plant clinic summed up successful planting as—

        1) judicious choice of site,
        2) proper planting procedure,
        3) planting in good soil,
        4) reducing weather stress.

The hedonistic delight I take in all the sights and smells, tastes and feels my garden gives me influences my choice of judicious site in the direction, wherever possible, of sensual enjoyment. Garden rapture was deliberately cultivated in the past when pleasures were less sophisticated and was largely accomplished by placing fragrant plants in telling places. The walks at Mt. Vernon make me feel that George Washington was not all that staid as school books taught us to believe. I know he was a serious farmer (his copy of Tull's *Horse-hoeing Husbandry* was well thumbed and noted) and that he was a most proper gentleman. But I doubt he would have had his walks edged with mignonette and pinks and cowslips if he did not sensuously respond to the fragrances that rose in voluptuous clouds when the ladies' skirts brushed against them on their evening strolls.

On May nights I am carried away by the lilac's scent gusting through my bedroom window. The lilac was there when I came, an ideal placement for pleasuring and prospering. It cares for itself in the sunny corner where the north wing of the house joins the courtyard fence nicely shutting out the sea wind. Yet for all its ideal location, had it been poorly planted it could not have grown so quickly from the bush it was into the tree it is. It would be hard to say which is the more important—the planting or the placing. A plant given a favorable location but planted poorly will be as unhappy as one planted properly in an unfavorable location.

We have in our yards minor climates within the major one, microclimates caused by sun and wind exposures and by slopes and frost pockets. I worked out the wind problem here by noting how Nature works out hers. Where only a few soft-leaved violets hide here and there among the iris in the open meadow, they spread into purple pools at the feet of the wild roses. And the roses shelter in front of salal whose tough leaves intercept the wind, turning it aside if it cannot be broken. I also noticed how many wild flowers and berries make their home in the high shade and protection of the broom thickets. Inland gardeners who cannot shield their plantings from the wind with tough-leaved natives can usually find windbreaking shrubs or trees in most nurseries that will shelter and enhance the beauty of the garden.

The freezing wind and sun that play havoc with exposed winter-active perennials usually damage budding growth on trees and shrubs wanting to rush too quickly into spring. The overhead protection that saves easily-covered plants is almost impossible to give boughs and branches breaking out with tender leaves and flowers, defenseless because of height. Some of the damage can be reduced, some even averted, by a thoughtful choice of site. South and west exposures, where the temperature rises rapidly with the sun and drops abruptly at sundown, encourages premature flowering,

growth and disaster. In cooler locations, dormancy is prolonged; the air warms gradually and cools gradually; and the reduced light checks the urge to emerge too soon.

Plants have ways of communicating their preferences. The majority of perennials we grow bloom in late spring, summer or fall and generally want more sun than shade. If there is more shade than they like they will leaf too much and flower too little. Then there are the very-early-blooming evergreen perennials that want more summer shade than sun. Their urge to flower in late winter and early spring is spurred by the increasing light of lengthening days. So they enjoy all the cool spring sun they can get but want protection from the hot summer sun by way of high shade, dappled shade or shade in the afternoon. But like all flowering plants, they need sun enough to keep leaves and flowers in balance.

These are mainly average plants coming from average climates in the North Temperate Zone. But many of us grow plants from higher elevations in this zone, and from altitudes of 2 and 3 miles bordering the Tropic of Cancer. Yet these plants, bringing with them their exotic beauty and fragrances from alpine meadows and mountain slopes, settle happily where sun, shade, and water satisfy their needs.

Among these European and Asian immigrants are members of the Primula family and they taught me the ABC's of plant language. Their leaves and roots spoke clearly of conditions in their homeland and I can see no reason why this instruction should not apply to other plant families coming from like environments. For those who have tried and failed to grow these stunning plants of dramatic origin, my observations on roots and leaves in relation to sun, shade and water may be of interest or help.

Those with fleshy roots and large, thin leaves want relatively little sun but plenty of water. To further protect themselves from the sun, their flower stalks and the underside of their leaves are sometimes heavily powdered with gold or silver meal. Their fat roots never had to work for food or water in the deep, rich, permanently moist humus where they flourish in their native Himalayan stands. They feel at home around semi-shaded pools, along stream banks, in moist deciduous woods, and in shadier garden spots where the soil has been mellowed with humus and can be kept watered in the summer as well as dry springs and falls. They are used to wintering under deep snow so, even though many are herbaceous, an airy overhead protection is advisable if the temperature drops below 25° F for any length of time and there is no snow cover.

Plants with much smaller leaves—often thick and sometimes leathery—and thin roots speak of hardship among rocks in open, stony fields common to the European Alps. Their flower stalks too can be coated with gold or silver meal as can the underside of their leaves. I have watched such leaves turn their underside to the sun and so follow it to protect the unmealed topside. Or, instead of meal, some have developed a hairiness or a fuzz on their leaf undersides and stalks to intercept the sun's direct rays. Their roots are wiry and tough from drilling into the thin and stony soils in search of food and water.

Though their leaves speak of life in the sun, the plants usually seek shade in the hot part of the afternoon by rooting among rocks or in their crevices, or wherever some relief can be found. They need a readily drained gritty soil, lean but with some humus, and occasional deep soaks in the summer to duplicate the heavy showers of their mountains. Some furl their leaves into spears in the winter, others with very small leaves do nothing but sit quietly and let the snow cover them. Since they are used to this protection, they appreciate a light, airy cover when the temperature drops below 25° F in prolonged snowless periods.

The average plant is happy in a basic loam which is a combination of sandy or gravelly soil, clay and humus. Plants originating in rocky situations want this soil sharpened with rock chips and a rock chip mulch under leaves and around their neck. Plants from wetter regions, accustomed as they are to large amounts of decaying vegetation, want more humus. To achieve a basic fertile loam is not difficult. Everyone can supply the humus. And it is easy to open clay and keep it open with fragmented rock. But for the overly loose or gravelly soil the only permanent cure I know is the addition of clay. If the gardener with abnormally open soil could only exchange part of it for some of the clay in another's garden, both soils would become living loam as soon as the humus went in.

Clay is the Cinderella of the soil. Misconceptions have disfigured the true beauty of its character. Lucky is the gardener with clay because clay is so much more than rock particles. It is totally mineral composed of many minerals in the soil-forming process. So fine are its particles that an electron microscope is needed to reveal the fact that each one is flaked or layered like scales on a fish. This creates such a vast surface that there is an acre of area in one quart of clay. Think of what this means in terms of electrical attraction. Consider the amount of surface for attracting and holding every nutrient except nitrate and sulfur. Humus attracts and holds with its larger particles, but humus is quickly recycled in thin, highly ventilated soil so its binding effect is short lived unless constantly replenished. Only clay is permanent.

I learned about opening clay with small sharp rock after the nursery's careless man dumped several barrow loads in one end of a pollinating bench and left it there. He was to have spread it over the entire bench floor for drainage but, instead, mixed all of it with the filler soil in a very small area. The new Cowichan strain of polyanthus primroses, scheduled for that section, had always been a scanty seeder. After two months of pollinating what could be called a forest of sturdy stalks, the plants were lifted and fielded out to develop and ripen their seed crop which matured into pods fat beyond believing. In those two months of bench life, each single crowned plant had expanded into a large, vigorous clump carrying a mass of new roots which clung with bulldog tenacity to the little jagged pieces of rock. This suggested tilling about 3″ of rock chips into the heavy creek-bottom soil where all seeding plants spent their confinement. The opening and airing of the packed, clay soil stopped the crown rot and stem rot which always before had been a serious problem. The miracle continued year after year without further applications.

All sand and gravel companies sell this fragmented rock which is called ¾″ minus because the chips measure from ¾″ down to particles. Sand is usually recommended to open clay, but mason sand packs and coarse concrete sand is only a boy trying to do a man's job. Hardpan is also quickly and permanently opened with ¾″ minus. This insidious condition can lie concealed under a layer of good soil and be the unsuspected cause of poor growth no matter what is done for the good of the plants. Hardpan is like a floor through which air, water, and roots cannot penetrate. It is brought about by walking on or working the soil when wet, by the weight of building equipment, but more often by years of shallow digging. Only deep digging exposes it.

Hardpan needs breaking up only once if ¾″ minus is used in the breaking process, and if the addition of humus and deep cultivation are continued. The full bite of a fork or spade is about 12″ when sunk straight down to the haft and this is a good air depth for root growth. Those who fork or spade on a slant could be working only the top 6″, or less. This habit of shallow digging has persisted over the years. A wise old Victorian lady laid down a maxim worth remembering: "If mother earth is well fed and if you have got her deep down, and not a surface layer of half a foot on, she will take care of every plant you commit to her hold".

So if, when digging straight down, the tool meets resistance before it can take a full bite, you have met hardpan. A pick breaks up this hard floor easier and better than a fork, but a fork is the best tool to pound the lumps into smaller ones, mixing them with the topsoil as the digging proceeds. When the smashing and mixing is finished, spread dolomite or ground limestone over the top, no more than 4 quarts for 100 square feet. This amount will barely cover the soil yet is a good 10 pounds. Over it all, spread from 1–2″ of

¾" minus depending upon the heaviness of your soil. Work the rock chips and the calcium-carrying material throughout the soil and water gently but well.

Fork humus into the upper half of the worked area if it is to be seeded or planted at once or within a short time. Otherwise let the soil weather without the humus until planting time nears since air and calcium together encourage rapid recycling. If the humus pile had several light layers of dolomite, ground limestone or wood ashes while it was building, one direct application of a calcium-carrier should be enough for reconstruction. It is the ¾" minus that keeps the soil open permanently. Once opened, continued deep digging, humus, and the earthworms it brings transform hardpan into deep down, full-bodied loam.

Some of the planting procedures about to be suggested may seem unorthodox but they grew out of my experience at Barnhaven where many problems had to be solved along with those that others brought me. I became a great coddler of roots, before and after planting, whether the plant was moved from one part of the garden to another, or whether the material was purchased bare root, canned, or balled and burlapped. I also came to believe that the time to plant is best guided by the plant's rhythm, the seasons, and the feel of the earth.

Planting in cold climates, I believe, is best done in the spring as soon as the soil can be worked rather than fall when the ordeal of winter lies ahead. We all agree that planting in warm climates should be done in fall or winter. In indecisive climates, such as the Pacific Northwest and most of England, too many perennials, shrubs, trees and roses planted in the fall winterkill because of premature growth during the mild periods followed by sudden freeze. I find spring planting very much safer. Winter dormant trees and shrubs are best moved when limbs are bare and hibernating on the food stored during their active months. But when such stock is purchased for fall planting, ask if the leaf drop was natural or artificially induced for earlier sale. Evergreen trees, because they never go completely dormant, should be spring planted in cold or indecisive climates when growth buds are swelling, and fall planted in warm climates after the year's growth has ripened.

Spring flowering broad-leaved evergreens such as rhododendrons, camellias and the like, move best in opening bud or bloom when they are semi-active. Perennials can be planted or transplanted from one part of the garden to another in the spring after the last hard frost, soil permitting, to about six weeks before fall frost. Soil permits when a small amount squeezed in the hand falls apart when pinched. If it sticks together it is still too wet to work or walk on.

When planting fever is upon us we may not always remember to visualize how big the new addition will be in a few years. Growth begets growth and each plant, bush, shrub and tree needs enough headroom for a free play of light and air if it is to remain healthy and beautiful. Nothing encourages aphids and fungus more than crowding, particularly among the thinner leaved. It is also easy to forget eaves, especially when planting in good weather. Plants made to stand under the drip or back where rain cannot reach, will soon reflect in their tops the lack of air in the wet position and the lack of water in the dry.

Whether the plant is new to the garden or relocated, the hole should be prepared with equal care. It should be very much wider and deeper than the roots at planting time to accommodate future growth. I am generous with the humus when mixing it with the soil taken from the hole. And again I mention using about 6–8 quarts of steer manure mixed with the soil and humus in a large hole, about 4 quarts in a smaller one and, for plants, a double handful or two. In heavy soil I would dig some ¾″ minus into the floor of the hole and add enough to the planting mixture to guarantee a free flow of air and water.

Never include fresh manure or inorganic commercial fertilizer in the mixture going back into the hole. Nor should it be placed below the roots where it could burn on contact, or leach out of eventual root reach and be of no use at all. Such material is reliably safe only when put on top of the soil after the plant shows signs of growth. It is then able to absorb the nutrients in amounts small enough to handle. Scatter commercial fertilizer sparsely, turn it under about an inch, then water well so that the concentrated nutrients will reach the roots greatly diluted.

Perhaps my greatest break with planting tradition was made when I learned the effect a hardened ball of earth has on the roots of plants that have been dug for some time. The success of my seed and plant crops depended upon observation—finding the reasons for good or bad behavior. One very poor seed crop uncovered the cause of disappointment which, in turn, uncovered the reason for the mysterious failure many were experiencing when planting balled and burlapped trees and shrubs.

The routine of transferring primroses from the field to the pollinating

95

benches and back out to the seeding area disclosed a wretched root condition. Pollinating stock had to be selected and dug in early spring at which time the soil was saturated and mucky. After spending about two months in the benches, this particular crop was lifted and fielded. Each clump had hardened into a cement-like ball through which no root had penetrated. For these two vital months the plants dwindled in poor health for lack of food, water and air. Every spring thereafter I manipulated each clump—whether sticky from the field or hard from delayed planting—before it went into the benches. I took the clump in both hands and, with thumbs holding the top of the ball, pulled it apart from the bottom with my fingers so that the roots could freely grow into the bench soil.

Nurserymen must dig and ball their stock for fall and spring sales when the soil is very wet otherwise it could not cling to the roots. We are told not to break the ball and, usually, not to remove the ball's degradable wrapper when planting, that the roots will grow through it. But after my experience I could not see the roots penetrating the hardened ball, and certainly not continuing on to penetrate the wrapping. Roots start to grow about a week or 10 days after planting and in that time the wrapper could not possibly disintegrate. So I advocate removing the wrapper but do not suggest deliberately breaking the ball though I can see no harm should the ball accidentally break while being planted. Its sole mission was to keep the roots in contact with the soil and that duty ends with the planting.

If the ball is dry, soak it in its wrapping for a few hours before planting—some say overnight which could be too long for the good of the roots. Allow it to drain awhile, then place it on the soil mixture in the hole so that the top of the ball is level with the surrounding surface, or a little above since it will settle with the watering. I would then unfasten the wrapper, slide it out from under the wet ball, then pierce the ball here and there from top to bottom (and the bottom too) with an ice pick or carving fork.

While filling the hole, keep tamping the mixture around the ball for a solid set. When about ¾ full, and the ball is holding fast, give it a very thorough soak. Then add more mixture and firm down gently until the top of the ball is level with the surface—or slightly below surface for a shallow catch basin—after the final deep watering. Keep it well watered before and after new growth begins. The roots will need this help for some time to feed and anchor the plant.

When planting bare root, the following four fundamental principles will help the plant establish and grow more quickly:

1) Keep the material to be planted out of the sun and wind and cover the roots with wet gunnysacks or the like, or with the nursery wrappings which have been removed and kept wet.

2) Cut off any dieback, the black or dark colored part of root ends and branch tips. Pruning shears and storage probably account for these dead ends from which no new growth can emerge unless cut back to healthy tissue. Use a sharp knife for cutting because the single blade cannot bruise. Last March I experimented on a rose shipment by cutting off a tiny bit of all roots at the same time I cut off the

dieback. The first crop of blooms several months later was bountiful; the second in September and October was phenomenal. I now gently root prune all plants going into the soil to stimulate root growth and bloom just as I do when cultivating established plants.

3) Never bend a root when planting for a bent root, like a bruised root, will die. In positioning shrub, tree, or plant, make sure that every root is spread straight out or straight down. When shaping the soil mixture into a cone in the middle of the hole for the plant material to sit on as I do with roses, see that the roots are well spread and hanging down, unbent. Always there should be plenty of soil mixture below the roots and to the sides for growing room.

4) Make sure that soil and roots are in firm contact since it is difficult for roots themselves to make contact in loose soil. After planting, test for a solid set by gently pulling. If the plant does not move, all is well. If it does, or lifts out, keep firming the soil until it sits solidly.

Since water is vital for plants to establish, a shallow catch basin is helpful to collect water and check runoff. Should the weather turn warm or windy when new leaf growth is tender, give an overhead spray several times a day. When the new addition is growing well, loosen the top inches of soil and lay on enough humus or other soft organic material to bring it level with the surface after it has been watered.

Before moving plants from one part of the garden to another, water deeply the day before digging so that roots and soil cling together. Whether it is a perennial, a tree or a shrub, push the spade, shovel or trowel straight down, never on a slant which butchers the roots. All should be taken with a good ball of earth. If the ball is sticky, pull it apart from the bottom as previously mentioned. And if the roots are in any way exposed before planting, cover them with something wet.

Larger trees and shrubs are best left to professionals. When moving the young or moderately sized specimen whose branches spread, garden experts tell us to dig midway between the trunk and branch tips but I am sure I take a larger ball than this. Semi-spreading and columnar varieties give us no such gauge but, when in doubt, more root is better than less. All of this is best done on cloudy or damp days when there is little or no wind and, of course, in the best season according to climate and plant.

There comes a time when perennials need dividing. Their leaves and flowers diminish in size because the multiple-crowned clump can no longer adequately support the plant in what has become a tenement situation. Spring blooming perennials are best divided immediately after flowering or when new growth is just beginning. Summer and fall blooming plants divide best in early spring when still dormant, or when leaf growth first appears. This timing gives them all the longest undisturbed period for growing and storing food for the next flower crop. It also gives the longest possible growing period before fall frost.

Every year at Barnhaven we divided thousands of primroses, mainly to perpetuate named English varieties that were several hundred years old. I see no reason why the fast and safe way it was done should not apply to other plants. First, do not water the clumps before digging. After digging, wash or gently hose the soil from the roots so the clump will easily pull apart into single, double or triple crowns depending upon your purpose. (Whether you wish to increase your stock or whether you want a more showy display in the garden.) If the clump does not pull apart easily, cut between the tightly clustered crowns with a sharp knife making sure that each division carries good root support. Continued thin slicing for quick increase has lost many an irreplaceable plant.

After separating, cut back the roots of each division to the width of the hand holding it—about 4". Again use a sharp knife. Next, cut off the obviously old leaves even if new growth has barely started or not started at all. Toss each trimmed division into a pail of water as you work. Lift them out when finished, cover with a gunnysack or something similar, and take them to their freshly made beds for planting.

Divisions go into the prepared beds very quickly. Grip the trowel in one hand like a dagger, thrust it to its hilt (6") and pull forward. With the other hand drop the roots straight down into the hole so that the crown is level with the surface. Hold it there, and with the troweling fist ram the soil back hard against the roots. Low planting causes crown rot, high planting prevents crown rooting. Cultivate the knack of positioning so that after a good watering-in the plant's top sits neatly on the surface. Finally, test for firm contact by pulling gently on a leaf.

Many of the familiar plants we grow without a thought were brought out of China and Japan in the 19th century at great personal risk. While some

men were gambling their lives for gold, plant hunters were gambling theirs to bring us the living treasures we assume were always here. There was only a handful of such men and they either worked alone or with native helpers. China and Japan in those days were not easy countries to get into let alone get out of with plants and seeds. Yet one of the truly great collectors of that time— and all time—went into the wildest, most dangerous parts of China disguised as a native and brought out almost 200 species and varieties new to the Western world. It is hard to believe that many of the plants we grew up with and know so well today were exotics little more than 100 years ago. Certain roses and lilies are among them, azaleas, Forsythia and viburnums— and chrysanthemums, peonies, clematis and bleeding hearts. Nor can we in any way believe the horrible suffering and hardships endured to find and bring out these plants.

The 19th century plants of Chinese origin came from areas roughly corresponding to that of our states which are neither the most northern nor the most southern. This circumstance, coupled with average altitudes and fairly average rainfall, prepared them for the average garden here and elsewhere. After the turn of the century, the first few decades brought a flood of new plants out of upper Burma, southwestern China, and eastern Tibet close to the Tropic of Cancer but at extremely high altitudes.

This great circular area became the flower basket of the temperate world. It gave us magnificent rhododendrons with pastel or brilliant blooms shaped like bells or trumpets or flaring like lilies. Many of our commonly grown hybrids originate from these species. Oriental primulas beyond believing now live in our cool, moist gardens—pagoda shapes sparkle with silver meal; flower bracelets of every color but blue circle tall stalks; pendent bells swing in the wind dispensing heady spiced fragrances. Sky blue poppies, iris, gentians, lilies, magnolias, camellias—all of these and many more have brought us celestial beauty from a strange, unknown land. It was the plant hunters' paradise and in it the greatest of them all is buried.

George Forrest collected there on the high slopes of the Himalayas between 1904–1932 when he died on location. Though others had worked the area before and after him, he brought out the bulk of new plants and seeds. Most of these men were British whose expeditions were sponsored by the great seed houses and horticultural societies of England and Scotland. A few were French priests who had dotted their missions here and there on the lower elevations and gathered seeds from the heights when time permitted. All of them experienced excruciating miseries of terrain and climate working, as they must, between 2 and 3 miles up to get plants hardy enough for our northern latitudes. Often the stinging, cold, summer-monsoon rains turned to snow and covered plants before seeds could be picked. And always there was the hostility of the Tibetan lamas.

For years I have been haunted by George Forrest's account of his 1905 escape. He was a matter-of-fact Scot not given to fantasy, superstition, or even orthodoxy, and he gave little thought to the miraculous circumstance that saved his life on that first trip in. Instead, he lamented the loss of the 2,000 plant species, and the seeds of an additional 80 species—almost all of them new to the outside world—which he and his 17 native assistants were packing out when attacked. Somewhere along the way two priests and their 60 converts had joined the party. Thirty lamas in full war paint, with their women trackers, had been hunting them for eight days and nights when the miracle of Father Dubernard occurred.

During that time almost the entire band had been picked off with poisoned arrows, or had drowned themselves in the torrents, or had been slowly tortured to death. Forrest was preparing to make his last stand when he noticed Father Dubernard farther up the mountainside waving him on downstream. After making his escape this way he learned that the priest had

CANDELABRA PRIMROSE

died three days before the signaling. He also learned that Father Dubernard had been unspeakably mutilated before being dismembered while still living, and his parts distributed among several lamaseries.

Forrest died 27 years later when he was almost ready to pack out for the last time. This was his seventh journey, and though not yet 60 he intended it to be his "final run". He wanted to write about the flower fields he loved where "In the morning. . . . the sun as it touches the tops of the Mekong Divide, sends wide shafts of turquoise light down the side gullies to the river which seems to be transformed to silver". But his work was over. His Chinese helpers gathered armfuls of white roses and twined them into a wreath for his grave, white for their mourning.

10

Seeding Secrets

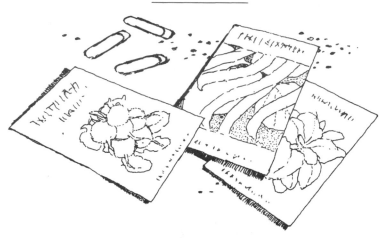

As the curtain dropped on the drama of plant and seed hunting in the Himalayas it rose here on the specialty nurseries, specialty plant societies, the Men's Garden Clubs of America, mushrooming women's clubs, garden magazines and books. Each maintained the other. The spiraling interest of the clubs and societies supported the specialty nurseries; the specialty nurseries supported the magazines with their advertising; and all supported the rising flood of gardening literature.

This was in the 1930s when I became a seed specialist. Little was known at that time about the behavior of seed and how to prolong its life. Germination was usually poor and garden writers, who knew nothing about seed, poured out many positive words on the subject of viability. They had no way of knowing that poor germination, or failure to germinate, was not the fault of the seed but the seedsmen's improper picking and storing of it. Many growers unwittingly picked green seeds along with the ripe and no immature seed will germinate. Some believed that poor germination increased sales and were deliberately careless in the picking while others were accused of drying their crop in the oven for a percentage of loss. Certainly no one I knew stored their seed after careful picking, curing and shelling in airtight containers at low temperatures.

Primroses were a rarely grown novelty in this country when I imported seeds from England and began expanding the limited color range of red, yellow, bronze, white and violet to a spectrum of colors, shades and tints never before seen or imagined. Primrose seed then was notoriously difficult to germinate, a year's wait for a spotty emergence was not unusual. But I soon proved that full germination could be brought about in a matter of weeks when the seed had been properly picked, cured and stored airtight at around 40° F. Cold storage is now generally recognized in the trade, and home gardeners with any kind of seed on hand—flower or vegetable—will do well to keep it refrigerated until time to plant and waken the life within sleeping so soundly it scarcely breathes.

From the time the pollen grain thrusts its maleness with unerring aim into the softness of the female ovule, conception is remarkably like our own. Many of our garden plants and fruits consummate the act between the rising and setting of the sun. And with consummation, the petals—once lovely in their shameless seducing—begin to fade and fall, and the embryo starts developing the characteristics of its parents. And like our mothers, the plant mother in her own way nourishes with her body the evolving life clinging to her placentas. As the embryo develops, each in its own soft envelope, she surrounds it with food and oxygen against the time it must leave her care and sustain itself until it can emerge in soil and sun.

After the seed ripens and is dropped or picked, the outer layer of this soft membranous skin enveloping the embryo and its packed stores begins to harden into the protective seed coat. Within this ever-hardening case the infant plant lies entombed, barely breathing. As it awaits the time to germinate and grow, its breathing slows to imperceptibility as the stored oxygen is used and carbon dioxide builds. Finally the tiny life lies suspended in anesthetized sleep.

Scientists now believe that the encased embryo could survive indefinitely on the food stored for it were it not for protein deterioration and respiratory failure. When moisture, air and warmth penetrate the seed coat before the seed is planted, the embryo responds as it would to normal germinating conditions and absorbs the stores its mother packed for its first rooting and leafing. Consequently, when the seed is planted the food and oxygen have either been used and the infant is dead, or not enough remain to support it until it can root and support itself. The life of certain short-span seeds has been prolonged as much as 50 times their normal expectancy when

kept dry and airless in cold storage. Long-lived seeds sleep safely for years.

When we put seed into the soil we know that it needs moisture but often overlook its need for oxygen. We are inclined to sow vegetable seeds too early and too deeply and one or both can cause suffocation. When we sow too early and the rains continue to saturate the soil, the seeds do not rot and die because of the wet itself. They die for lack of oxygen which the wet soil excludes, and then rot. When we sow too deeply, the shoots have to push too far and too long to reach light and air. They simply run out of food and oxygen before they can emerge.

The old rule of thumb is to cover seed 4 times its diameter. Some seed packets recommend sowing as deeply as 8 times, which really buries it. We should remember that seeds in Nature's garden fall from the plant and sprout where they lie with no hand to cover them. I find that peas and beans germinate faster when I cover them no more than ½", which is twice their diameter. And I barely cover small seeds such as carrots and lettuce. In this way the seeds get air even in wet weather, and they have only the minimum distance to push before reaching the light. We can always water the soil, and we can press the seeds back and cover them again if they surface, but we cannot puff air into it.

Keeping the soil moist reaches far beyond softening the seed coat. As soon as the embryo feels the moist touch, enzymes begin converting the packaged stores to availability. Insoluble starch becomes soluble sugar, insoluble proteins become soluble amino acids, insoluble minerals become soluble chemicals. With the energizing the embryo bursts through the softened walls. It twists this way and that as the infant root dives into the earth, obeying gravity. The shoot defies gravity and unfurls its green sails in the sun within a few hours of liberation. Then the newborn plant begins to breathe on its own after its own fashion. And with its breathing, all parts and agents integrate into a smoothly working whole. This is birth in the green world.

At no time are germinating seeds and seedlings more dependent upon a brisk circulation of air and water than when grown in flats or pots under controlled conditions. Without it damping-off fungi can wipe out an entire planting in a few hours. At Barnhaven I grew some 200,000 seedlings a year in two sowings for transplant sales and field stock. They were grown in roofed but otherwise open sheds which were loosely circled by young alders, thickets of wild plum, mock orange, wild roses and other natives on surrounding primitive areas. So I had to learn how to propagate in an air-retarded pocket. What I learned held all the simplicity of a miracle.

After losing two benches of germinating seed to bread mold and damp-off one spring, I began sowing as close to the bench top as possible for the greatest air drift around the seed and the necks of the newly germinated seedlings. The lath shade frames that I hung up in the early afternoon, I took down in the evening so that the night breeze and cool morning sun brushed across the benches for the longest possible time. And I learned to use little more than an inch of seeding mixture over a deep benchful of ¾" minus for air play around the roots and a speedy drip-away of water.

My next lesson came with the near loss of a summer crop of transplanted seedlings which had begun to rot. I found that the drainage cracks in the standard flats had swollen shut with subsequent waterings. With brace and bit I bored holes here and there through the soil and bottoms of more than 1,000 flats. I next had miniature railroad tracks of 2 x 4's laid, and the flats elevated across the rails for quick drip-away and air circulation. I then cultivated the young transplants with a carving fork as deep as it would go and saved the crop with oxygen.

I did not know then that I had also enlisted the help of the antibiotic producers. With air flowing vertically through the soil, top to bottom, and horizontally above and below the benches and flats; and with water passing through and dripping free, I had created an environment attractive to the benevolent disease-fighting soil families.

For those who are not familiar with damp-off (often called wilt) and how it works, there are 30 varieties of malign fungi capable of causing the disease. The most common one strikes seedlings near or at soil surface during the time their necks are tender. When seed is sown too thickly and the tiny seedlings are crowded together, drops of moisture collect in the forest of necks. Too much shade, poor air and water circulation—either one or all—add greatly to the already unhealthy crowded condition. When damp-off hits the tender seedlings they collapse as though scalded.

A number of fungicides have long been offered for the pre-treatment of seed to prevent damp-off. Before I discovered the preventive and curative powers of oxygen, I tried one of them and killed two benches of seeds. Perhaps I did not dilute it more than instructed. Or perhaps primrose seed is allergic to this particular fungicide. Whatever caused the disaster made me fear fungicides, soil drenches, and fumigants from that day to this.

As for steam sterilizing all the soil mixture that went into the seed benches and seedling flats, I simply was not equipped for it. Since then I have learned that certain soil families multiply their numbers more than five times within a few days after soil sterilization. So what is the point of it if air and water circulation remains sluggish enough to attract the malign disease-producing families. Sterilization alone does not guarantee immunity.

The principles of seeding are simple. Properly picked and stored seeds cannot help becoming healthy seedlings when air and water circulation is good, when there is a cool sun sweep, and the seeding medium is not nutrient rich. A lean seed bed is needed for germinating seeds and infant seedlings since they can use only the food stored for them until their first true leaf appears soon after emergence. There is a choice of lean seeding mediums: those with soil, those with no soil and no nutrients, and those with both. The old standard soil mixture is loam, peat moss that has been thoroughly soaked and drained, and coarse concrete sand—the three mixed in equal amounts. This mixture has enough sponge to retard drying, and the air and water circulation is fairly good but I often add a little ¾" minus for more openness.

Packaged soil substitutes are sterile and usually nutrient free. There is bagged vermiculite, mined mostly in Montana and South Carolina, which is mineral in origin. It retains some of these minerals (including magnesium and potassium) though it has been heated to around 1800° F. Another popular soil substitute is perlite, a volcanic rock exploded like popcorn under equally high temperatures, which carries no minerals. Vermiculite's platelike structure is similar to that of clay and holds large amounts of water which perlite cannot do on its simple, smooth surface.

Since I have not used soil substitutes I consulted a nurseryman who does. He relieves vermiculite's drainage problem by mixing it with perlite in equal amounts. He sows his seeds on this dry mixture, barely covers them with vermiculite, and then places the flats in a soak tray. He waters by seepage instead of overhead to avoid washing the mix around which can bunch or bury the seed. He also believes that water coming up through a dry mix anchors the seed better than sowing it on a wet mix. After a thorough soak to wet the medium and anchor the seed, he transfers the flats from the soak tray to elevated 2 x 4 tracks which provide the necessary air and water drainage. I have since learned that an expert amateur, working independently, devised this same seeding medium and soaking procedure and will use no other. I am anxious to try it next spring.

Home gardeners have devised mixes of their own. Some use equal parts of soil and perlite, some mix soil with vermiculite. The vermiculite mix would improve with some coarse sand or ¾" minus, or perlite. Sphagnum moss used to be a popular seeding medium but is seldom used any more. Because of its water holding nature coarse sand or sharp rock mixed with it should be an improvement. I have used straight Canadian sphagnum after pre-soaking and draining, packing it firmly up to the top of a shallow flat with very wide drainage cracks. It was a good germinating medium but like all unfertilized soil substitutes the seedlings had to be transferred to a fertile mix as soon as the first true leaf appeared.

Seeding containers should be chosen for maximum air and water circulation. Generally available are small, shallow trays with a screen-like bottom; also, 6- or 8-cupped units which fit into trays for small amounts of seed; there are peat containers which will rob the mix of moisture; and around the house are small cans which need only drainage holes punched in the bottom; plastic pots; and the old-timers' wooden flats. For my small sowings here I use either plastic pots with 4 or 6 large holes around the base or in the bottom, or flats with wide cracks or bored holes. I fill the scrubbed container with ¾" minus to within 1 or 2" of the top, making sure the drainage holes are not plugged, then finish filling with the old standard mix.

Soil mixes should be tamped down with a brick or any heavy object to bring the particles together and establish water flow between them. After tamping, add more mix and tamp again to bring it as near the top as possible for a good air sweep but with enough rim to keep the seeds from washing over the side when watered overhead. All mixes should be brought as near the top of the container as safely possible.

When sowing seeds there are no choices. They must be scattered very thinly and to do this I have always used a watchmaker's tray. It is a plastic triangle (sides 2½" and depth ¼") and may still be available at watch repair shops. The seed flow can be fairly well controlled by holding it in one hand and tapping the wrist with the forefinger of the other. Seeds should be barely covered if covered at all. I still leave seeds uncovered until germinated as I did at Barnhaven. (A ½" mesh screen laid on top of the benches protected them from birds.) In this way they can be watched for fungus or any troublesome development and then, if all is well, lightly covered with dry sand. A visiting Canadian nurseryman remarked that he had not seen this done since training at Kew.

Pre-treating hard-coated seeds to speed germination from months to weeks has become standard practice since the 1940 publication of my two methods. One uses hot water for watering in, the other imitates Nature by freezing and thawing the seed. Before these two simple and safe methods were publicized, the treatment in general use was scarifying, or rubbing, the seeds between fine sandpaper. This often killed more embryos than it delivered since a very light touch is needed and many gardeners, including myself, feel that if a little of anything is good, more is better. A few lighted a small fire over the top of stubborn seeds. As far as I know, the only other attempt to hasten germination was made in 1600 when Francis Bacon steeped some seeds in claret and some in a strong Madeira. It was not a success.

Only hard-coated perennials should be pre-treated which, of course, excludes vegetables and all other annuals living in soft coats. The hot water method is the simpler of the two. The water should be hot but not burning to the hand—between 115°–120° F gauged by an ordinary thermometer

HARVESTING PRIMROSE SEED

lowered into the sprinkling can. Then very thoroughly water in the seeds with your finest rose. When using a soak tray, give the overhead hot water application after the medium is wet and the seeds are settled in. Repeat once a day for the next day or two with 110° F water. Thereafter use tepid or cool water as needed to keep the seeding medium moist.

The freezing and thawing method grew out of watching one of my three old friends take her bottles of hard-to-germinate seeds into the high mountains every fall and abandon them to the elements for 4 or 5 months. Her years were considerably less then when she was populating her estate with plants, trees and shrubs from seeds received from Himalayan plant hunting expeditions. In the spring she retrieved the cache, still under melting snow, and sowed the seeds at once. All germinated magically and her plants have long attracted visitors from every gardening nation in the world.

When a perennial plant drops its ripened seeds in the warm months they either germinate at once to root before frost, or hang back waiting for spring. Those wintering over are subjected to periods of freeze and thaw which work on the hardened seed coat preparing it for germination as soon as the weather moderates. This action can be duplicated very simply in the freezing unit of the refrigerator. About 2 weeks before sowing, open each packet and drop enough water on the seeds to float them. Paper-clip the packets closed, bundle them together and wrap in plastic to keep in the moisture, then put the bundle in the freezing unit. Leave it there to freeze for about 3 or 4 days. As in Nature there is no set time. After this short period take it from the unit and, without opening it, put it on the kitchen window sill for a day or night to thaw. Then re-freeze, but first open the bundle and to each individual packet add a few drops of water to keep the seeds wet. (You will find that all or most of the previous amount has been absorbed.) Repeat the procedure once or twice in a 2-week period—more or less—however, seeds will germinate in the freezing unit if left too long.

On the final thaw be prepared to plant them. Open each packet and let the seeds dry at room temperature just long enough to allow them to roll free, usually less than an hour. Sow at once using tepid water for watering in. I once tried combining the two methods on primrose seed that had been in cold storage for 10 years. After freezing and thawing, I sowed and watered in at 110° F. Germination began the following day and continued quickly and evenly into an embarrassment of seedlings since fielding space had been reserved for only a spotty emergence.

The mechanics of transplanting seedlings from their sterile or lean mixture to a feeding mixture are basically the same as the preparation for seeding. Scrubbed pots or flats should have wide cracks or holes; planted containers should be elevated for air and water circulation in a good air sweep; and I still put ¾" minus in the bottom before adding about 2" of a good growing mix. This is tamped down, filled and tamped again to just below container edge.

For the growing medium, many use the sacked potting soil that is organically blended and weed free. I still use the standard seeding mixture, substituting leaf mold or fine humus for the loam. A small amount of steer manure is mixed into it—not more than a double handful to a bucket the size of a paint pail. Tiny seedlings are unable to handle rich food. Concentrated fertilizers, both organic and inorganic, have brought many a struggling seedling to a quick end.

Some gardeners transplant before the first true leaf develops which is necessary only when the seeding medium is sterile. The seed leaves, which precede the true leaves, cannot take up nutrients from the soil. These fat little leaves (the cotyledons) existed in embryo form in the seed and carry the food that was stored to see the infant on its feet. After this food has been used, the true leaf will provide from the soil and sun but must have a source of supply. If the seeding medium contains some nutrient, transplanting to the growing mixture can wait until several true leaves appear. I must admit that I would take little joy in tweezering out and tweezering in seedlings newly born.

When lifting seedlings with true leaves, loosen the soil with a carving fork or ice pick to prevent root breakage, but loosen and lift only a few at a time to avoid drying. My dibble is a forefinger wearing a fingerstall and I make a hole deep enough to take the roots hanging straight down. The hand holding the seedling positions it with crown at soil surface while the dibbling finger and thumb press roots and soil gently but firmly together. Space to allow for leaf development, about 2" between and across.

As soon as each container is planted, water in or tray soak. Then check the crowns to see that they are neither covered nor sitting high and, finally, test for a firm set by pulling gently on a leaf here and there. Shade them for a few days, then give them sun in the cooler hours, increasing sun exposure slowly to harden them off into strong and bushy transplants. Repeating: Elevate and keep them moist but not wet. A light surface cultivation with ice pick or common kitchen fork a few days after each subsequent watering keeps the roots moist longer, the necks dry, increases air flow, and generally stimulates growth.

If insecticide-fungicide dusts are used, little more than a touch is needed for control, more invites disaster. Such products should be diluted with some spreading agent, technical talc if it is still available at drug stores. Three tablespoons of the inert spreader mixed with 1 tablespoon of dust is safe and effective. Aphids can go unnoticed until transplants suddenly look very sick. They crowd on the underside of leaves, sucking away the plants' life, so it is the undersides that should be watched and dusted when necessary. The mixture stores well in a tightly covered glass jar.

Because glass does not draw moisture as plastic does, use only glass jars with tight-fitting lids when cold storing seeds. A quart jar holds many packets and takes little room in a corner of the refrigerator where the temperature stays around 40° F, never freezing. Scientists now believe that low temperatures either destroy some chemical that inhibits germination, or generate one that stimulates it. This may be, but long experience has taught me that airtight, dry, cold storage prolongs the life of the embryo, and without a living embryo no seed can germinate.

Though my seed orders are small and usually vegetable, I prefer buying direct from a reputable seed house in the winter when catalogs arrive. By early ordering the seeds are guaranteed some time in cold storage which benefits them all as well as having them on hand when soil and weather are right for planting. Always there are more vegetable seeds in a packet than I can use in one sowing. I paper-clip these packets of leftovers, date the sowing and return them to their jar in the refrigerator. I draw on them for repeated sowings in the weeks ahead and continue to draw on them over the next year or two as long as they last. They always germinate as well as fresh seed.

The life expectancy of vegetable seeds varies surprisingly. Members of the gourd family live the longest—8–10 years for cucumbers, melons, pumpkins and squash. Cabbage and its relatives—turnips, broccoli, Brussels sprouts and cauliflower live up to 6 years. Pea seeds have this same life span. Beets, radishes, lettuce and spinach can live from 3–4 years; beans, carrots, corn, parsnips, onions, peppers and tomatoes have only 2–3 years.

We all know that cool weather vegetables such as peas, salad things, root crops, and the cabbage family pay no attention to a light frost, and packet directions generally tell us to sow as early in the spring as the soil can be worked. But there are springs when the rains come after planting and continue until an oxygen problem exists. If the seeds have germinated and the leaves begin to yellow, try to give them a light cultivation. They usually begin to green and grow after air reaches their roots. I know that not everyone can cultivate from path, lawn, or street as I do, but when it is necessary to step on wet soil loosen your footprints with a digging fork as you back away.

I find that even cool weather vegetables reach the table sooner when I do not lose my head and rush out and plant the first time the young spring sun comes out for a few days. Certainly warm weather vegetables such as beans, corn, cucumbers, melons and squash must wait until the soil is warm and mellow and the rain falls only when and as it should. Squash taught me the truth of this by dying before it could germinate. Fresh bean seed planted in early April took more than a month to germinate and then the young plants sat there yellowing, doing nothing until I cultivated them. Year-old seed, planted in May the following year and warm-watered in at about 90° F, began to germinate in 5 days and did not falter on their climb to the top of the quince. I have since speeded vegetable seeds on their way with warm water after planting.

The practice of soaking pea and bean seeds a few hours before planting has been handed down from generation to generation, but I did not

pre-soak the year-old bean seed used in the May planting. Its success suggested a September pea trial. From a year-old packet in the glass jar I counted out 135 hard, wrinkled seeds. While they were softening and expanding in tepid water, about 2 hours, I counted out another 135 equally hard and wrinkled seeds from the same packet. After shallow planting and tamping, I watered in the soaked and the unsoaked with warm water (again about 90° F) and waited 3 days before checking. On the third day, 3 each had germinated; on the 4th, 7 each; on the 5th, 17 each; on the 6th, 47 soaked and 44 unsoaked; on the 8th, 67 soaked and 70 unsoaked; on the 19th day, a total of 73 soaked and 90 unsoaked had lifted their hooded heads into the light.

Though I no longer soak peas and beans, I do inoculate them with cultured nitrogen fixers. Garden shops and seed houses sell inexpensive packets of this inoculant—usually dated with the in-packet life span of the fixers—guaranteeing their presence on the roots of the peas and beans. Nitrogen fixers cannot always be relied upon to be in the soil where you want them. A certain number will have survived the previous harvest, but not one will inhabit soil where peas, beans, or some close relative have not grown the year before.

This black powder can be used in several ways. Packet instructions are to roll the seeds around in a bowl with some of the powder barely moistened with a few drops of water. I found that condensed milk instead of water coats the seed more heavily. Finally, I avoided the sticky slowness of planting wet seed by putting the powder in a large kitchen salt shaker and shaking it over the seeds after planting.

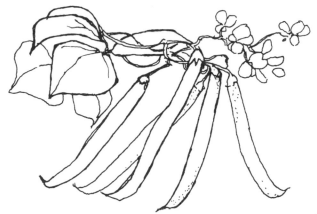

Recently the inoculant has been in granulated form which is easily scattered over the seeds in their rows. Use generously before covering them with soil and tamping. The more powder or granules used, the more nitrogen fixers there will be to convert free nitrogen to nitrate. The packet has always contained more inoculant that I could use at one time, so I paper-clip it closed, date it as I do the seeds, and put it with them in protective cold storage. They, too, live longer sleeping there in the cold jar.

Instructions can take longer to read than to follow, but once followed the procedure becomes simple routine. I believe that gardeners go through two phases when beginning their seed sowing experience. When I made my first sowing of primrose seeds I had never handled seeds of any kind before nor had I watched anyone to see how it was done. My excitement evidently outweighed my ignorance. The seed already bloomed in my hand so I was not afraid to try. Soon primroses from all over the world actually began to spring from the earth seemingly happy in my happiness. I could not believe that sowing seed and having plants grow from them could be that easy. Then my innocence deserted me and I became diffident and tried too hard. I approached them with all the anxiety a mother feels when faced with bathing her first child for the first time. Often the seed did not appreciate my elaborate preparations. After that phase passed I simply followed the path of common sense.

If you have wanted to raise plants from seed but have been timid about starting, buy a few packets of annuals which germinate quickly and easily. A few months after sowing the seed you will be enjoying their bloom—touching them, smelling them, cutting them for every room in the house. I always have a bunch of something in the refrigerator to pleasure me whenever I open the door. There is the color and fragrance of Swiss meadows and English hedgerows, oriental flutes and temple bells, wild mountain slopes and valleys—the whole world in a jug.

Or put a few vegetable seeds in the ground, any sunny spot will do. And when you have finished, you will feel closer to the land taking joy in the fresh-turned soil and the spring shower, alone with yourself and the good seeds and the good earth. Sowing the soil brings an intimate feeling of being at ease in the midst of everything—not sophisticated riches but very satisfying.

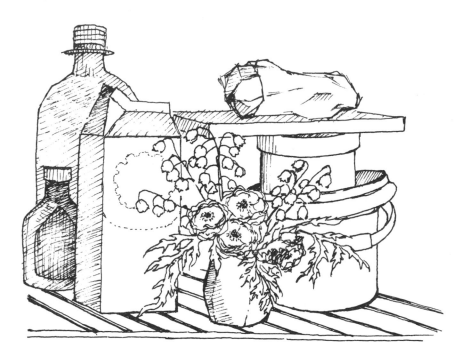

11

Table Talk

The night is very warm and very still and the harvest moon has set a great silver platter on the dark blue tablecloth of the sea. I stand and let the silvered dark absorb me and think back on the gardening year, almost over now. How pleasant and productive it has been. And how fortunate I am to have escaped the commercial conditioning that has made so many focus their attention on pathological possibilities causing them to do things better left undone. Even wise old gardeners can pick up the habit. I was surprised to hear one of my ancient friends say the other day, "I have lost the stars. All I see is the trouble I am looking for". Plants want only what Nature gives them— the amount of sun or shade they like, air around their roots and tops, water, and the residues of life—and for us to stop fussing so much.

Every one of these priceless commodities is free. No longer do I accept the gifts of sun and air and rain without conscious gratitude. No need to ask where we would be without them. And without the residues and discards that put flesh on the bones of our soil. Flesh that feeds, shelters, air conditions, defends our plants' and soil families' health, and conserves water. Though the rain is free, stored water is not and it is well to remember that one deep soak on soil with a well-padded body is worth six sprinklings on a skinny one.

Frequent sprinklings are more aggravation than help to plants. Light watering cannot activate the pumping system that circulates air and water to the deepest roots and forces out the accumulated carbon dioxide. Scientists say that the average plant asks for water when it begins to wilt during the hot part of the day. They claim that if deep rooted plants are allowed this low moisture level for a short time before giving them a deep soak, more flowers and fruit of better quality result. And that a dry summer, like root pruning, produces heavier crops. Fruits and berries are sweeter in a dry season because more sugar is made in sunny weather. In rainy weather less sugar can be made but leaf growth flourishes as roots take up more fertilizer with the water. When the growing season begins to taper off in the fall, plants wintering in colder climates should not be watered unless absolutely necessary. Freezing temperatures are less hard on them when their parts are not swollen with water.

As to when to water, there is a running controversy between evening-waterers and early-morning-waterers, each convinced that their timing is the right one to prevent leaf spotting. I water whenever I please guided by my plants. No spotting has occurred other than on those leaves which have served their purpose and are preparing to die naturally. When either leaf spot or yellowing is not part of normal decay it is, as we know, caused mainly by lack of air around tops, roots, or a need to activate the pumping system.

Here, where summers are often fanned by high winds, leaves transpire abnormal amounts of water even from vegetatively mulched soil. (Forestry experts say that a full grown broadleaved tree gives off a large barrel of water on a hot day without taking into account the wind factor.) So I water in the late morning or afternoon or whenever the wind is at its highest. I give everything, including roses, a long overhead shower to help the leaves better stand the torment of the wind. After all, Nature showers everything without favor in spring or summer from a cloud floating in a sunny sky.

Watering is one of my garden pleasures. It is a time for relaxing and noticing and ministering. Often I carry pruners and as I soak the soil I cut off dying flowers and stalks that are beginning to seed, directing that energy into new growth. Or prune away proliferating rhododendron branches that interfere with such treasures as the Sky Blue Poppy of Tibet. Or cut spent rose canes to stimulate food intake and divert it to the swelling stem buds for the coming bloom. Or do nothing but enjoy watching a rose-pink ranunculus bend over and lay its turbaned head on the shoulder of a tulip.

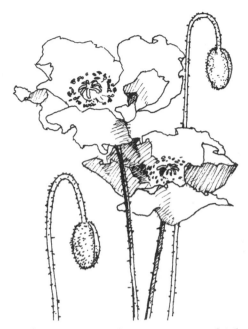

Rotation is another subject of controversy which need not concern gardeners who renew their soil with organic matter. Even at Barnhaven I grew the same crop every year for some 30 years in the old orchard on the hill despite prophesies of doom. For one thing, there was no other extensive fielding area. For another, the soil was remade every summer with strawy dairy manure, and with the petals, leaves and apples falling from the trees.

Rotation was practiced from Tull's time into the 19th century to deliver crops from their own excrement. Tull based his rotation theory on his belief that plants ingest, digest and defecate. A turnip crop, for example, failed because the previous year's crop had fouled the soil. However, this turnip excrement was of great benefit to, say, grain or potatoes or pasture crops. And the excrement from these crops benefited the following turnip crop. Since Tull did not favor the use of animal wastes and knew nothing of vegetable waste, his crops did need rotating just as do crops today where there is insufficient organic matter to rejuvenate the soil.

If rotation was necessary in my garden I could not continue the intensive planting that I do here. Coastal conditions and limited space do not allow much change of location. At first I wondered if the young peas and beans would need full sun before they could start their climb into the branches but found that intensive planting is not the same as crowding. A plant is crowded when it must compete for light, air, food and water and loses the struggle. In the summer growing season the sun rides high and its rays reflect into places which are out of reach at other times. This makes it possible to grow a surprising number of vegetables among light shrubs or under deciduous trees which allow sun at their feet.

When we left the vegetable seeds sleeping with the nitrogen fixers in the refrigerator, we also left a fascinating part of our past. Our ancestors' destiny was greatly shaped by the kind of food available and its abundance or scarcity. If they had land to work, grains and legumes were their mainstay. And it seems that wherever life congregated, there some legume grew to provide protein with its seeds. Lentils are one of the oldest cultivated foods and were a staple in early civilizations—"Jacob gave Esau bread and pottage of lentiles" in Genesis. Peas have been ladled, thick and thin, into the bowls of Europe and Asia for thousands of years.

Beans also are an ancient food but those the early Egyptians and Europeans grew bore little or no resemblance to the kinds we cultivate. We never think of Columbus as an enthusiastic plant hunter but he introduced into Europe many exotic seeds and plants from tropical America, among them were green beans. Whatever the cyclic behavior of plants in their native hot climate, they are warmth loving annuals in cold climates. But yet these beans spread over three continents, being slowly improved, before the French Huguenots brought them to North America about 100 years after Columbus had taken them from South America. As for lima beans, we did not start growing them until the first half of the 19th century. One of our naval officers brought them from Lima, Peru, some 12° south of the equator, and began cultivating them on his New York farm.

When contemplating the journeys of beans, I have wondered why it took us until this century to start growing soybeans. Chinese and Korean farmers had developed more than 1,000 varieties over the past several thousand years which, as we know, gave them 22 grams of protein in every cup they cooked. Perhaps this was because no early plant hunter brought them out before our traveling botanists did. Since their introduction, we have developed numerous varieties to suit varying climatic conditions but even these need summer warmth to mature.

Some of the cabbage family—which takes its name from *caboche,* the Norman French word for head—offers a protein surprise. Though cabbage itself carries only 2 grams per cup when steamed (1 when raw) broccoli, which Italian gardeners developed from cauliflower, contains 5 grams. Brussels sprouts, first seen in medieval Brussels, provide 6 grams. Spinach, with its 3 grams per cup, came to us with the earliest settlers having first found its way to Europe from ancient Persia. Radishes, onions and garlic, which I am never without and which I have come to respect for their antiquity as well as their pungent, flavorful qualities, were purchased for the builders of the Great Pyramid more than 5,000 years ago.

Carrots are a vegetable of all seasons so constantly before us we give no thought to their origin. They were first brought from Persia to Rome in the early Christian era and from there spread throughout Europe. When we come upon the wild Queen Anne's Lace in the fields or along roadsides, we are looking at the common ancestor of all varieties grown today. Carrots give us only one gram of protein per cup but over 18,000 units of Vitamin A. Spinach is a runner-up—almost 12,000 units. Steamed dandelion greens provide 27,000 units, the highest Vitamin A content of all edible plants. These lowly greens, these lawn and garden pests, also deliver 5 grams of protein per cup if we want to pick and steam the leaves. I have eaten dandelion greens in Southern homes and they taste better than they sound. I have also drunk the South's dandelion wine made from the flowers and raisins, and learned that its golden blond look of innocence in the glass masks a deceiving nature.

In the beginning, when I hoped for a promised pair of artichokes and visualized other vegetables and strawberries growing in my landscape, I said that I would report on the harvest. A number of seasons have come and gone since then bringing riches to my table, my purse, and my soil. The artichokes, with their leaves of silver and their great purple thistle-flowers exceeded all expectations of beauty and delicate flavor when their great globes were cut and cooked at once. They do not bear heavily for me because they miss the hot summer sun of their Mediterranean homeland. But if they never bore, these majestic vegetables would pay for their space in silver. I know they bear well inland, and authorities say they produce in climates as cold as Massachusetts if they are covered with a basket or wooden box when the temperature drops below 28°F. But the basket or box is not meant for protection serving only as a frame to keep the overhead mulch, mounded over the top, from pancaking down on the crown and rotting it.

I learned that small seedlings of the old tried-and-true vegetables move without complaint if they had been too thickly sown, so I transplanted the crowded zucchini and crooknecks, Brussels sprouts, carrots and spinach to suitable empty spots. When the spinach was ready I did not pull up the plant but kept cutting the leaves which stimulated more leaf growth. And when signs of seeding appeared, I cut off this tasty tender part together with some of the leaves but left enough on the stem to keep the plants growing. In their frustration to seed, the plants kept trying and I kept cutting young leaves for more than two months. Meanwhile, edible-pod peas did double duty behind the roses growing along the street side of the courtyard fence. After producing pea pods by the pound they fertilized the roses and the daffodils over which they had been planted.

Squash is far richer in romance than protein—summer varieties only 1 gram per cup, winter varieties 4 times that amount. No one had to bring squash with them when they came because it had always been here. The Massachusetts Indians called it *askutasquash,* meaning vine-raw fruit, and it was generally eaten from the Northeast to the Southwest. Some tribes used the great golden blossoms in their religious rites and culture. The popular squash blossom jewelry, still being crafted by some Southwestern tribes, goes back to the time, not so long ago, when Hopi maidens wore their hair in side coils resembling squash blossoms to proclaim their virginity.

Because hybrid corn was developed from Mexican maize it loves warm days and nights when, mid-westerners say, you can hear it grow. Of course it never could be happy here on the coast but in other parts of the country it is in almost every vegetable plot. Just thinking of corn, freshly picked and steamed in the husk in the oven, puts sugary juice in the mouth and 5 grams of protein in every cupful of kernels eaten. Corn and other cereals—classified as grasses and the earth's most important family—must depend upon the willy-nilly blowing of the wind for pollination. Because of this haphazard way of mating, Nature is open-handed with the gold dust of fertility. From a single corn tassel the wind flings millions of dusty pollen grains in all directions, sometimes toward another's silks, sometimes away. The gardener can help in the union by planting corn in double rows, or in spaced groupings of four or more. Or the plant can be self-pollinated by shaking the pollen-bearing tassel at the top of the stalk over the flower-silks below. There will be no sterile blanks on the cob if every silk can winnow from the wind, or otherwise capture, a pollen grain for itself.

Cereal grains have been feeding us and our animals for over 5,000 years and now our breakfast tables know them in a palatable wealth never before imagined. In addition to these gilded staples of our ancestors we have the glamour of perfected fruits, berries, and aromatic beverages—the romantic teas and the coffees that lure us out of bed in the morning. Around the edges of this aroma I still can smell the unforgettably sweet fragrance of white coffee blossoms penetrating the chilly morning air in the highlands of New Guinea. Cocoa and chocolate appeal to sweeter tastes—chocolate for those who like it rich with fat, sweetened, and flavored with vanilla; cocoa for those who want it unsweetened and with most of the fat removed.

We know that both chocolate and cocoa are prepared from the seeds of the cacao but little is generally known about these bewitched trees. While in New Guinea I was the guest of a cacao planter whose 200-acre plantation was on an island near the equator off the east coast. It was harvest time—one of the three main ones that occurs during the year—and the pods were the size, shape and texture of acorn squash but seldom green. They were orange, red, rust, purple, yellow, magenta—ballooning on the brown trunk and branches of a single tree. A hand could have reached into a basketful of dyed squashes and flung them at random at the tree where they stuck to the bare bark at odd angles.

When fully grown, cacaos are about the size and shape of filbert trees with flowers resembling babies'-breath. This creamy pink, flowery film breaks out in a spotty rash on the main trunk often 3″ from the ground and continues, here and there, up the trunk and out on the main laterals. The tiny

flowers erupt throughout the year and are pollinated by ants and other small insects. Three months after pollination the seeds (about the size and shape of almonds) are fully developed. I can think of no place more exotically enchanting than a cacao grove in the South Pacific.

Even so, my heart belongs to the temperate zone where I feel more at home with the quiet turning of the seasons and the wide choice of plants offered me. My seacoast summers deny the ripening of fruit but if I lived inland I certainly would have dwarf peaches and nectarines (the fuzzless peach) apricots, plums, pears and apples. I would have them mainly for their fruit, of course, but also for their beauty in all seasons—the bare shapeliness of them in winter which spring drapes in scarves of soft, scented silk; their large flushed fruits redolent in their ripening; their leaves coloring for the fall. They give so much and ask so little room, yet that small space could support peas and beans as well. And these in turn would fertilize the little fruit trees just as they do my beautiful but barren purple leaf plum.

All this flowering and fruiting is such a soft and beautiful way of surviving. It is not for us that the fruits and berries are so often brilliantly colored and aromatic and delightful on the tongue. The sweetness of the flesh and the color of the skin is an invitation to the birds to come and feast and scatter the seeds far from the bearing mother for their own place in the sun. So we and the birds together eye the ripening, waiting for the sugar content to reach its highest level. It is the picking at sugar peak and eating soon after that makes the home-grown fruit and berry so deliciously superior.

Nor is the sweetness of the freshly picked vegetable meant for us. The plant makes this sugar daily for its own use and the future use of its offspring. What we call the sweet taste of the earth is glucose at its peak caught before its conversion to flat-tasting starch granules. Only when pod, ear or root is taken when young and tender—when it has not yet completely matured—is the sugar content still building. When reproductive maturity has been fully reached, the sugar is stored as starch. But why the sugar begins to lock into starch as soon as the young and tender are separated from the mother plant, or the soil, I do not know unless it is a natural but hopeless response to the need to survive. This explains the loss of flavor in vegetables which have been harvested and left lying around at home or on the produce counter. Only those who grow their own produce can enjoy the almost 25% peak sugar content of such vegetables as peas when picked while young and cooked at once.

And only the home gardener can grow the tenderest, juiciest varieties of fruits and berries, kinds that cannot survive commercial handling and shipping. I am thinking now of strawberries because many bowlfuls of fragile, juicy-ripe berries have come from the plants which at first grew only

in my mind. Uncounted varieties have come and gone in a steady stream ever since some long forgotten European produced the first commercially important strawberry early in the 18th century. He or the bees crossed a wild form from this country, Virginia most likely, with one grown by the Chilean Indians. But years before this, English cottagers grew local kinds and city dwellers traveled miles into the country for strawberries and clotted cream. Dr. Boteler was one of these strawberry fanciers whose name would be forgotten too had he not said better than anyone since, "Doubtless God could have made a better berry, but doubtless God never did".

It is easier to keep birds from the ripe berries than it is to curb the exuberance of the plants. Their straw-like runners (from which they take their name) root so promiscuously that my original 25 everbearing plants have populated every sunny spot in the neighborhood. Surely there could be no better ground cover. Should birds become a problem, I will follow the strategy of an English friend who simply stretches black cotton thread here and there over the beds. Nothing intricate is needed since the strands are invisible to the birds and trip them on contact. My problem was slugs until I placed a fairly high collar of scratchy wood excelsior under the leaves and rested the green berries on top.

In my hopeful beginning I said that I would gladly forego a crop of peas to see tomatoes hanging ripe on the vine. I have since found that I had to give up nothing to enjoy tomatoes from late summer to mid-winter. I have picked from one tomato plant, settled into the warmest most sheltered spot in the courtyard, nearly 100# of almost-ripe fruit which fully ripened after picking. I had given it several applications of Liquinox 0-10-10 three months after planting to check growth and hasten heavy fruiting.

The potted tomatoes—and peppers—on the window seat of the sunny bay window produced well into February. The black plastic pots I used were 8½" deep and 8" across though larger containers would have been better for the tomatoes. I filled the bottom third with ¾" minus taking care to keep the drainage holes open. (Only the other day I watched a bonsai master use rock in this way.) The mix for the top two-thirds I made spongy with a little pre-soaked and drained peat, open with a little ¾" minus, and nutritious with humus, good soil and some steer manure all thoroughly mixed. A little charcoal in the mixture worked wonders.

The pots, elevated on rock in their saucers for drip-away, were kept moist but not wet by watering thoroughly when at the drying point, never letting them stand in water. A day or two after watering, I cultivated with the ice pick sometimes piercing deep into the pot to break a few roots. Standard tomato varieties seemed to produce longer than the compact types but needed staking and tying. Unfortunately, aphids appeared out of nowhere (they were particularly fond of the peppers) so I took all the plants outside and gave them a firm blast of water on the underside of their leaves. This hosing, along with a breezy airing in cold but non-freezing weather, eliminated them.

Concentrated fertilizers of any kind often kill potted plants because the confined space increases the concentration. Many nurserymen and florists use Osmocote (18-6-12), a fertilizer that is encased in resin for slow release. The small beads are scattered on top of the soil around the plants after potting where it disperses nutrients over a period of months. I bought a small amount from the local garden shop for testing and found that the tomatoes and peppers I picked in February were from the pots that had been given a teaspoonful of Osmocote and lightly scratched in. Had the nitrogen content been less and the phosphorus more, I am sure that fruiting could have continued longer. The plant food spikes (14-3-7) available at my supermarket have been formulated for foliage.

About 150 years ago someone was courageous enough to eat a tomato. The Spaniards who followed Columbus brought these "love apples" out of Peru and were grown as poisonous ornamentals until someone took the first bite in the 19th century and lived. Many believe that a tomato's first blooms must be pollinated by hand before fruit will set. I was of this belief until I began growing them indoors out of the reach of bees. When I went to pollinate them I found that fruiting had already begun. The same holds true of peppers which, surprisingly, are shrubs in their native hot climates.

You may have noticed how alike tomato and pepper and Irish potato blossoms are but did not know that all are closely related members of the Nightshade family. It is hard to believe that the old table wife we call the Irish potato has an exotic background. It is not Irish at all but a tender South American which English explorers introduced into Ireland in the 16th century. In the 18th, migrating Irish brought it to North America where it thrived and brought more Irish in the mid-19th when blight caused potato famine in their homeland. The so-called Irish potato reached Europe not long after Columbus introduced the sweet potato whose South American name, *batata,* attached itself to the Irish potato probably because of the edible tubers both produced. But in no way is the Irish potato related to the sweet potato. For that matter, the sweet potato is in no way related to the yam.

"Plant ye first the potatoes" is an old English proverb. Nothing opens the soil like potatoes shouldering one another around for growing space. It is best to begin with seed potatoes from feed stores, or from garden shops which sometimes carry them in the spring. Lacking this source, ask a farmer or fellow gardener for a start. Potatoes from the produce stand are usually treated with a growth-inhibiting hormone to prevent sprouting and are apt to yield little more than disappointment. After your first harvest there will be enough small ones from each crop to plant the next. When dug, store them in a cool dry place, always covered since the light turns them green and bitter.

A medium-sized potato, baked or steamed, gives us only about 2 grams of protein. But think of the ways potatoes delight us—I can count 16 from baked to pancakes. Delicious as they are, accompanied or alone, they are memorable when gathered one minute and steaming in their jackets the next. I do not dig them all at once in the fall but gather as I wish over the summer, taking them like eggs. And the satisfaction is the same when I reach my hand under their leaves into their nest and feel around and take a big one here and there without disturbing the others. My potatoes are not always without blemish but gathered this way and cooked with the sweet taste of the earth still in them they are perfection. Always, as long as I have a garden, there will be potatoes in my landscape.

12

Creative Reproduction

Gardeners seem to have a particularly deep-rooted sense of the beautiful which swings from the spiritual to the sensual and all degrees in-between. We are enraptured by a flower, catch our breath when we hear the song of a bird or see a butterfly or a rainbow. There is a feeling of ecstasy in the soft kiss of a breeze carrying fragrances in mysterious blends that cannot be described or forgotten. This aesthetic communication between gardener and garden is an integral part of total gardening, yet I believe that the ultimate heights are reached only by making excursions into creativity.

When you plant seeds that bear the stamp of your own hand your thoughts are in full bloom the year around. From one year to the next your imagination is kindled with possibilities and the need to know what you and Nature have brought into being. In creating something that did not exist before, life seems to extend beyond its limitations, even to a sense of immortality in the lasting beauty of your work.

There is nothing obscure about selecting plants and pollinating their blooms by hand. Only the literature about it makes it seem so. Amateurs continue to create outstanding varieties in their backyards. Needed, only, is love for the chosen flower lighted by imagination and observation. These are the true requisites. The mechanics are simple, the underlying principles are simple since the sexual habits of most plant families are usually quite staid. The variance lies in your selection of mates for the nuptial rites. Romantic, unplanned marriages performed by the plants' natural lovers brings forth children of chance. Planned plant marriages remind me of old-time oriental elders who chose man and maid for family ties and to reproduce superior children without waste of generations. It is selection that has brought about this century's dramatic leaps in producing greater beauty and quality in plants and animals.

Since the beginning of life on earth, Nature has been the mother of us all. Out of her developing body we developed and so formed our bond of oneness which links every living thing together in the Great Chain of Being. Though the green-blooded and the red-blooded families have gone their separate ways, never has she failed to provide the basics for our physical and sexual survival. Over eons of forgotten time she herself has had to adapt to many changes, as often violent as gentle, and in so doing devised various means of continuance for each species of her children. Some of these devices have long since been abandoned because life continues on the upward swing of development. Methods of procreation which served in those lost periods of time are of no use to life as it exists today.

In this age of flowering plants Nature has become a canny match-maker. She is determined to marry off every last daughter in the bloom of youth to produce progeny and carry on the family line as far as possible into the uncharted eternity ahead. Should a daughter fail to attract a suitor, some unique methods of sexual performance have been contrived. One of the most ingenious plans to avoid spinsterhood is the ability given most flowers to reproduce themselves without a true nuptial ceremony—where bride and groom are born, love and die in the same blossom. Plants much prefer an old-fashioned consummation with their natural lovers but should bird, wind or insect fail in the nuptial visit, then self-marriage is better than no marriage at all. This is called self-pollination.

One of Nature's mysteries that is beyond our comprehension is virginal reproduction—the development of an egg without fertilization which occurs in both green and red worlds. The name given this phenom-enon (parthenogenesis) is from the Greek which combines 'virgin' with 'genesis', or virgin source. Even more remarkable is the fact that insects and plants reproducing in this fashion do not lack sexual equipment. Who would suspect virgin reproduction in the voluptuousness of an apple orchard in full bloom. And yet some varieties do produce fruit by pollination without egg fertilization. And so it is with pineapples and bananas, which do not seed, together with the seedless varieties of citrus fruits and others. In the animal world, aphids and males of the bee families and their relatives are examples of virgin reproduction.

This sexual regression produces exact duplicates just as vegetative (asexual) reproduction leads a plant down a blind alley where no change for its betterment can occur. There is only a bleak chance that, for one reason or another, a sudden departure from the parental type (mutation) may occur and break away from the dull, inherited monotony of sameness that endlessly multiplies the non-mutants. Sexual reproduction alone provides unlimited possibilities for enriching and diversifying the progeny of both the rooted world and the mobile.

But there are times when vegetative reproduction is needed to duplicate plants that do not set seed or to maintain, without change, a valuable plant. I am thinking now of the potatoes I grow and those you eat—if they are white potatoes—which are all descended from the one plant young Burbank developed more than 100 years ago. And of double-flowering plants such as primroses, some of which are hundreds of years old. Neither Burbank's potato nor double primroses set seed so all are the youngest surviving parts of the old individuals.

In addition to tuber increase and multiplying plants by division of the parent, gardeners add to their stocks by offsets, grafts, cuttings and scales. With her typical inventiveness Nature is more fanciful. There are plants with trailing underground roots which produce new plants. Some species have rhizomes—large, fleshy underground storage appendages rich in food to support new growth. Others, such as my strawberries, populate their surroundings with runners. My lilac's suckers need constant pulling. Some oriental primroses develop aerial plantlets from spent flower heads, while others encircle their dessicated remains with a new family.

Bulblets huddle alongside my lily bulbs like chicks around their mother. And little black bulbils, in an overwhelming show of zeal, sit alone or in twos or threes, in every leaf axil along the 5' stalks of the Tiger Lilies now in an excess of bloom. They drop and roll and root everywhere—along the street, over the courtyard fence, among the peonies—these shiny black lily children are always underfoot.

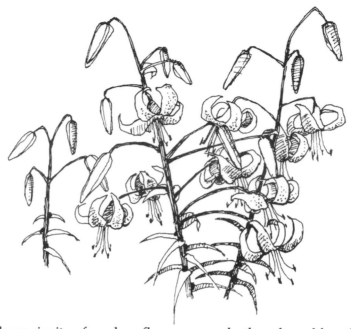

The majority of modern flowers carry both male and female organs in the same floret (dimorphism) and are considered the perfect flower type. Here Nature outdoes herself in strategy to ensure pollination by one means or another. Though cross-pollination is preferred she has devised some 20 ways for a flower to fertilize itself should all lures fail to attract pollinators while she is receptive. For annuals, which bloom and die the same year, it is absolutely necessary for species survival. Without the safety belt of self-pollination, annuals would perish from the earth in the year of their unfertilized bloom should cross-pollination fail en masse.

Though self-pollination is a needed back-up measure for survival, it is cross-pollination that holds the key to the evolution of plants as is the sexual selection of the female among insects, birds and animals. Superior quality in fruits and vegetables; greater beauty, vigor, and seed production in flowers; endless possibilities for variation—all these advancements result from cross-breeding. Two parents are certainly better than one, but one is better than none.

To accomplish cross-pollination, Nature has contrived various ways and means. One is self-incompatibility which makes pollen impotent to fertilize the ovules of its own flowers but compatible when coming in contact with neighboring flowers of the same species. Some plants, under cultivation, develop strains that differ in sexual character—one strain will be self-fertile while another will be self-incompatible. And some flowers have been constructed in such a way to make self-pollination impossible leaving no alternative but cross-pollination.

Cross-pollination in some plants is ensured by having the pollen and the stigma mature at different times. The pollen either ripens and is shed before the stigma becomes sticky and receptive. Or the pollen is kept from ripening and shedding until after the stigma has lost its adhesive ability to hold, nurture, and spark the pollen grains on their way to the ovary. The time lapse between pollen shedding and stigma maturity ranges from an hour or two to several days. Certainly the intelligence that guides this planet is far beyond ours to comprehend.

The most significant aspect of our linked lives is the shared function of sex adapted to the state of mobility or immobility. Despite appearances, the organs designed for procreation in the red and green worlds are essentially the same. The pollen—which corresponds to the sperm of animals—fertilizes the ovules in essentially the same way. When the procreation period ends and allure has served its purpose we, like the flowers, lose the freshness of youth.

The sex organs of flower families are arranged in various ways. The simplest is the single structure used by members of the primrose (*Primula*) family. In the heart of each bloom is cupped the ovary filled with unfertilized eggs (ovules) with the style connecting it to the stigma above. These three

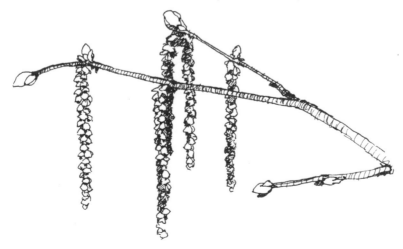

parts compose the pistil—the female reproductive organ. The male organ, called the stamen, consists of anther and filament, the filament attaching the anther to the petal. The anthers cluster closely around the stigma of primrose blossoms, sometimes above it, sometimes below, encasing the pollen and holding it tightly until mature, then releasing its fertile load. This is the invitation to pollinators to come and tumble around in it, to coat themselves with it before flying off and brushing it wherever they will. However, when the pollen is carried above the stigma much of it falls and the flower pollinates itself. The mission of the calyx is to hold in protective embrace the immature reproductive organs within the bud.

When self-pollination occurs, consummation time varies from the immediate to days—about a day for corn, tomatoes more than two, five for cabbage—even weeks and months for some non-flowering trees which are pollinated by the wind. Each pollen grain becomes an independent plant of sorts as soon as it leaves the anther. Though we cannot see it we can rely upon the word of botanists who tell us that this organism breathes in its own way, thirsts and hungers as do visible plants. It lives only to reach and fertilize the ovules. Every assistance is given it since it may survive only a few hours or, perhaps, a few days. In very rare instances it can survive for a year.

Where pollen is concerned, Nature is an out-and-out spendthrift. But with the entire green world depending upon this fragile speck of life to carry out the male's role in sexual union, niggardliness would bring quick disaster on us all. At least one pollen grain is necessary to fertilize each ovule in the ovary, in some instances hundreds are needed. The pollen grain's journey begins when it reaches the receptive stigma glistening with female fluid. Its stickiness holds this infinitesimal bit of male, quenching its thirst while nourishing it with a sugary secretion to activate it. After activation, a thread like projection develops and grows down the style—teased along by exciting chemicals excreted by ovules and stigma—until it reaches the ovary, then drives on to penetrate the egg. On penetration, the tip of this projection releases two nuclei and, with them, half the destiny of its kind. And again, as with us, the ovary/womb begins to swell with the new life it carries.

These fragments of popularized botany for gardeners who, like myself, have fought shy of formal presentations, may bring you closer to the green world. Just knowing how alike we are could be the spur needed to visualize new forms, new colors, new whatever-you-can-imagine in the plants of your choice. There are species to improve and their varieties to expand. There are hybrids beyond counting waiting to see the new finery you have designed for them. But the block put in your path by well-intentioned but ill-informed writers on the subject must first be removed.

Each seems to put his feet in the footprints of the previous writer repeating negative notions. Unintentionally they have diluted the inspiration of two men's work by complicating them. Were these simple men still living they would wholeheartedly agree. Great work often grows out of a simplicity that is not clouded or influenced by hard-set orthodoxy but is fed by imagination, acute observation, and logical conclusion. Neither of these men set out to revolutionize the plant world. Compelling curiosity drove them, a hunt for answers to their questions. Unfortunately, they have been pedestalled beyond our reach.

Not all of us can be a Gregor Mendel or a Luther Burbank. But they were men, just as we, who lived and loved in their own way. Mendel was celibate, a priest of the church. Burbank was not, having had two wives. But each had one consuming love—plants and the need to learn their mysteries. Both knew that every plant, like every child, holds within itself the seeds of uniqueness, that we all are the product of our genes and environment. Burbank worked on a wide screen, based largely on the distinctly different behavior pattern of the same species in differing environments. Mendel's work was, by nature and necessity, restricted to investigations on a small screen which eventually magnified a thousand fold for he discovered the fundamental principles of heredity and became the father of modern genetics.

Gregor Mendel was born (1822) in the Austrian province of Moravia, now Czechoslovakia, in poor circumstances. His peasant parents were poor, his health was poor, his chances for schooling were poor all in the face of a great thirst for learning. However, he did manage to finish his secondary schooling and attend a higher institution for a time, but declining health and dwindling funds forced him to leave for Brunn and take refuge in the Augustinian monastery there. As a monk he was freed of financial worries and free to continue his studies—which, at first, had nothing to do with the work that lay ahead, unthought of. Doubtless it was this fixed desire to learn that interfered with his post as parish priest from which he was shortly relieved and sent to the University of Vienna. After three years of natural history and mathematics he returned to Brunn and was placed in the parochial high school where he successfully taught science.

It was this particular choice of subjects that combined to fit him for his scientific destiny which he began to fulfill at once. No different from home gardeners, he had but a small piece of ground to work on—his plot being alongside the monastery building. Here he began his investigations into the laws of heredity by using 22 differing varieties of garden peas which, because of their normal habit of self-pollination, provided a clear-cut breakthrough when cross-pollinated. His eight-year study can be found in almost any book on botany, biology, or genetics. He had nothing more in mind but to satisfy a scholar's curiosity. In view of his natural self-effacement, he probably would have been embarrassed had he known the extraordinary impact his findings eventually made on the world of science.

But a strange and unfortunate coincidence kept his work gathering dust on a shelf in the abbey's library for 35 years. He published his findings in a modest paper which, in 1865, he read before the Society for the Study of Natural Science in Brunn. Here it stopped despite the fact that he had discovered the fundamentals of inherited characteristics in plants and animals that had baffled men for centuries. There is no doubt that part of the reason for its isolation lay in want of a translator to bring it out into the other languages of the world. But the primary cause was the publication, in 1859, of Darwin's *Origin of Species by Means of Natural Selection*. The storm of controversy it raised among scientists was still gathering momentum when Mendel read his paper six years later and it continued to rage, unabated for several decades, blinding the scientific world to other significant discoveries.

So botanists failed to learn that an unassuming monk, working with garden peas in a monastery garden, had answered questions and solved unexplained problems the great Darwin had raised. But at that time all branches of science were discovering so many answers to so many long standing questions in such rapid order that scientists must have had difficulty assimilating everything at once. It was not until the turn of the century that Mendel's paper saw the light of day having been discovered almost simultaneously by three scientists working independently. Before Mendel died in 1884 he experimented with other plants and bees but his scientific work came to an end when he was made head of the monastery. His life was good and true and pure as a fine bell struck.

As for Luther Burbank, he was not the perplexing wizard the press encouraged people to believe through stories exploiting him, stories which spread world-wide until they became a harmful thing. He was as crystal clear

as a mountain stream and as fast flowing. This transparency put him so far beyond the understanding of more devious minds that they missed the man entirely. Slivers of conjecture became logs that kept rolling, collecting myths along the way until man and myth became hopelessly entangled. It is true that he had no academic training, that he never read Mendel's principles of heredity though he was 51 when the paper was translated into English. His work was already in full swing at the time stunning horticulturists and scientists everywhere.

Until a year ago I knew nothing of Luther Burbank's life or work. But I have since become well acquainted with him, knowing him as a gentle man who was finely tuned to Nature. Recounted bits of this side of his character may encourage home gardeners to make their maiden flight into the magical world of hybridizing. My acquaintance began with a visit to his home and grounds in mid-town Santa Rosa on a trip through northern California's wine country. Quite unexpectedly I found myself in the 19th century and the middle of a centennial celebration. Men, women and children in the dress of a hundred years ago busied themselves with household chores in Burbank's modest cottage, greased axles and sharpened tools in the carriage house. Others, in Sunday best, strolled along paths that wandered over the grounds and under trees where apple juice was being served from large tubs, around the rose garden, and through the small greenhouse. Boys in knee breeches and girls in pinafores rolled hoops and otherwise amused themselves and visitors with the games of that day.

The celebration, sponsored by the Luther Burbank Museum, commemorated his purchase, September 13, 1884, of these 22 lots for $2,000.00. The framed deed hung in the carriage house close to the old upright piano discarded for the big square one which left limited space in the small cottage living room for the other furniture. His desk was there and on it lay an unfinished letter written in his rather fine hand. It was to a relative, as I recall, about his irritation with someone who had hauled so many loads of manure that he would be contending with countless flies for some time to come. This I understood since I had lived with loads of manure and flies. But I did not begin to understand the man until I chanced to happen upon his grave.

I had wandered away from the festivities to be alone and sort out my feelings for the place, then overwhelming me, when I suddenly came upon it in his front yard. The yard was very small, the grave midway between the cottage door and the white picket fence that shut out the street. It was only a scrap of lawn dominated by a giant Cedar of Lebanon under which Burbank lay covered by a piece of galvanized tin cut to fit. That is all—the piece of tin set in the lawn, the towering tree his monument, the earth absorbing him in death as it had in life.

Burbank was born in 1849 in Massachusetts where he turned to truck farming as a young man. He was in his early twenties when he came upon an Early Rose potato that had playfully decided to produce a seed ball—a most rare event which he never saw again. In the ball were 23 seeds from which he raised 23 plants, keeping only two from which came the then unknown white potato. It was the ancestor of all the Netted Gems (also called the Idaho Russet) which now outranks all other varieties in production, 14,000,000 bushels being grown annually on the West Coast alone. Burbank sold it to a Massachusetts seedsman for $150 and is said to have been on the train to California three days later.

In his late teens he had checked out of the local library Darwin's *Variation of Animals and Plants Under Domestication* which became his bible. He then purchased Darwin's *Cross and Self-Fertilization in the Vegetable Kingdom.* These two books—coupled with his intuition, curiosity, and powers of observation, his imagination and ability to select and conclude swiftly, plus his obsession with what he was doing—were the tools of his trade. He kept many of his records in his head or on anything that came readily to hand: wrapping paper, used envelopes and unused portions of their contents. He completely confounded dyed-in-the-wool scientists who worked in laboratories tracking down theories and recording every step. They considered both Mendel and Burbank amateur observers.

Of course they could not begin to understand Burbank's free thinking which orthodoxy would have killed. He was not shackled by tradition, he had not read that it could not be done. He quickly and confidently cut through the fat to the meat of the matter. Nor could they comprehend his need to make a living within the framework of his research. His advertisement in the Santa Rosa Daily Democrat, September 23, 1884, offering "500,000 vigorous Fruit and Nut Trees growing in our two nurseries at Santa Rosa. . . . DON'T BE FOOLED. . . . Come and See. Catalogs will soon be ready. Luther Burbank" made no sense to scientists whose work was confined to the laboratory.

By 1888 he had reached a point where, to all intents and purposes, he could quit the nursery business and devote his time to developing new varieties. But he continued to punish his body, never strong, always driving himself to keep ahead of the Juggernaut of his own making. He was up at daybreak and working shortly thereafter at his experimental farm seven miles away. Every summer day found him working in the heat tasting fruit, judging its over-all merits then returning home—his stomach churning with the acid consumed—to a yardful of visitors waiting to wring his hand. In other seasons he hurried along rows of ornamentals conning thousands of seedlings or blooms, selecting the best at a glance without second thought. Journalists and the idly curious expected him to be gracious despite the grueling schedule and all-consuming attention to his work. He was not.

Burbank created more than 800 varieties of vegetables, flowers and fruits, but had he originated nothing more than the Netted Gem Potato, the Santa Rosa Plum, and the Shasta Daisy he would still be considered the world's outstanding horticulturist. The truly learned men of science were nonplussed but supported him, the lesser belittled him. He was diffident by nature but confident in his work. He was bolstered by a sparkling sense of humor and an enthusiasm that remained alive until he died in 1926, a year he felt would see a number of nearly perfected varieties reach culmination. His life, filled with child-like wonder, was dedicated to Nature and her teachings. He looked with reverence on everything and everyone seeing all as members of the world household working together for the common good and a harmonious whole.

When I look back 50 years to my beginnings as a hybridizer it is hard to believe all that has since happened. The story I now relate has never before been told in this detail and I do so only in the hope that it will prove an incentive to others. Of necessity, my subject must be primroses but they well serve as a model from which to work no matter what flower family excites another's interest. I had no model to work from since what I did had not been done

before; I had never read a garden book—scientific or otherwise; I had never grown a plant but for some reason, still unknown, I had fallen in love with primroses. I knew nothing of them until I read a friend's English catalogs and, with my last $5, sent for the seed that intrigued me most. Now the Barnhaven strains of primroses, in various forms, are known and grown everywhere. They built the bridge that has spanned the distance between an English hobby plant and the high-powered primrose industry which flourishes world-wide today.

I have no fondness for personal disclosures so have never confessed that Barnhaven grew out of a fanciful dream. It happened the day I sat on a footbridge over the creek and looked, with stars in my eyes, at my first primroses blooming along its banks under the catkined alders. At that time they were the best available but in my mind I saw them in a Utopian world of color with series Americanized as the first step toward evangelizing them in this country. So the few bronze shades were thought of as the Grand Canyon series; the few reds as Indian Reds; the reddish purples were transformed, then and there, to the Marine Blues of purest hue; the yellows became Harvest Yellows for our ripening wheat fields; white, Winter White, for the fairylands of snow. This was, at that time, the entire color range of polyanthus, the bunch-flowered primroses. Now there are over 140 shades, fixed to come true from seed, the widest color range in their history and, I am quite sure, that of any other flower.

Color obsessed me. Years later an old professor friend told me that this was so because of a broken engagement with music for which I had compensated since tone is color heard, and color is tone seen. So it could be said that Barnhaven's hallmark is a triad of color, lilting grace, with overtones of fragrance. In my visionary world, where anything and everything was possible, it never crossed my mind that flowers could very well see things differently and not yield to dreams. But the green world can rise to noble heights and primroses proved to be tremendously talented. They put themselves without reservation into my hands.

Long after the Barnhaven strains had become horticultural history I was told that I had committed the cardinal sin of linebreeding. Linebreeding continues to produce new colors every spring at Barnhaven (now in England's Lake District) which, with the exception of one alien introduction in 1947, means that no outside blood has been introduced into the original parent stock over the past 50 years. Once again misinformation, spoken with authority, had been taken up and repeated until it had become gospel. Fortunately for primroses, I knew nothing about it having never heard of linebreeding. After enlightenment, and learning of the dire results this method of plant breeding purportedly produced, I consulted several books on genetics. I found that I had intuitively and logically taken the quickest route possible to improve the plants, to fix desired characteristics, and to produce hybrids that bloomed true from seed which, otherwise, is the prerogative of species.

Linebreeding is based entirely on selection of the fittest and other qualities that meet the visualized goal. It is used in animal breeding for this purpose, and was practiced by the Ptolemies through brother-sister marriages ending with Cleopatra, to perpetuate the desirable mental and physical characteristics of the line. Linebreeding, a form of inbreeding, ensures control of future generations, the progeny of each being chosen for superiority in every detail needed to reach the objective. When continued, each generation produces a larger percentage of desirable individuals with fixed characteristics from which selection can then branch out into altogether new and exciting byways.

It is Barnhaven's linebred strains that are responsible for the fantastic popularity of primroses today. The fixed colors, being dominant, continue to be used in Japanese, European, reportedly Chinese, and British Commonwealth admixtures transferring to them as many of Barnhaven's colors and forms as suit each hybridizing operation. Unfortunately, the built-in Barnhaven hardiness has not been maintained in many of these new strains now flooding the markets of the world. For the most part the new strains carry varying amounts of the Pacific Giant strain which, having been produced in the mild California climate, had no chance to eliminate the weak. From the beginning to the present, Barnhaven strains have been mercilessly selected by the weather, only the fittest surviving the repeated onslaughts of bitter freeze to produce equally hardy children the following spring. Since primroses are naturally a hardy outdoor flower, it is a pity that in cold climates these new strains overwinter in commercial greenhouses—countless acres under glass—leaving them with no constitution to resist even a light freeze.

When I conceived the idea of cross-pollinating my first primroses by hand I had to find a way to do it since it had not been done before. How simple it was to tear down a bloom and find that I held in my hands all the

BARNHAVEN—THE ORCHARD ON THE HILL

pollen, attached to the petals, while the female reproductive parts sat in the calyx, completely naked. What, then, was more obvious than to apply the pollen directly to the stigmas of those plants chosen to bear seed. By observation I had escaped the tediousness of the traditional brush with its slowness, the inefficiencies of sterilizing after each cross, the need to bag, and whatever else was necessary to do. Instead of each stigma being lightly brush-touched with pollen, my fingers transferred a heavy load making the seed set phenomenal. This thick coating, and the removal of the enticements of color and scent, made pollination by natural agents impossible. I had stumbled onto the technique of emasculation which proved to be the wings on which the operation flew and which has long since been adopted and used wherever hand-pollination of primroses is practiced.

Record keeping began with a simple system of labeling that has remained unbroken and efficient over the years of acceleration to mass production. It went hand in hand with the seasons from spring through summer, fall and winter, never ending. Each color series was labeled as was each shade making up that series. Seeds were sown, harvested, shelled, and refrigerated by shades. And beginning with the transplanting to flats, to fielding out, and back to the pollinating sheds—each color series was controlled by the labeling of shades. When selecting pollinating stock from the field I naturally chose the best to improve the next generation, and always among the best were plants of outstanding excellence. These I marked with one star or two stars, as judged, and when planting to the pollinating benches I kept them in starred rows, under their shade name, in their color series.

The pollen from this starred stock was first used to pollinate other plants in the starred stock rows and, since pollen supply almost always exceeded demand, it was then used on the unstarred plants which pollen was discarded unless needed. (I have since learned that Burbank assessed the worth of his varieties by this method of marking, using double crosses instead of stars.) As new shade breaks appeared, they were labeled and kept separate until they came true from seed. Only then were they included in the appropriate established color series. If they did not fit, another series was born, given a descriptive name and expanded. Eventually more new shades appeared in this latest series which founded still another—and, so, on and on far beyond those first daydreams. Every morning and every evening the aisles of the pollinating sheds were thickly covered with fresh primrose petals whose pollen had been used or discarded—long runners of tints graduating to shades and shades graduating to colors—a rainbow carpet woven by Nature and the hand of man.

This is the centennial decade of the modern garden polyanthus. Gertrude Jekyll of Munstead Wood, Surrey (England), is well-known for having first begun their development, releasing them in the 1880s under the name of Munstead strain which I bought in the 1930s. Her interest lay only in the white and yellow shades which have been carried on in Barnhaven's Harvest Yellows and Winter White—direct descendants which, after 50 years of selection and hand-pollination, are more robust, more beautiful in every way showing a proud pride in their ancestry.

Though "impregnation by hand", as it was called then, had been tried now and again in the 18th century, the rogueing method was still being used for commercial seed production. This was a slow process involving the elimination of unwanted plants as they bloomed hoping that the bees would cross, with thought, those left to bear seed. In the other method used, the best plants were staked and seed collected from these only. But I have watched bees at work and have come to believe that only the first flower or two in a bunch, or on a plant with many individual blooms, is cross-pollinated. The bee flies from one plant carrying its pollen to another. There it tumbles about among the flowers of the newly visited, very shortly coating itself with its pollen. The remaining blooms on that plant cannot help being self-pollinated. So Miss Jekyll spent from 10 to 15 years reaching her goal having started with two plants—a mottled bronze and a near-white from a cottage garden.

THE OLD BARN ~ BEFORE BARNHAVEN

Never will I forget my struggle with her nickel-sized orange polyanthus. The size of the other yellow shades had been increased until they quite ruffled out from around a silver dollar. This stubborn, stocky little plant, however, glared up at me, year after year, defying me to change its ingrained habit of pollinating itself in tight bud, ripe pollen and receptive stigma clasped in close embrace. I finally chose a large gold, used the pollen of the orange on it which produced, in the first generation, smallish golds. Then generation followed generation before the brilliant orange color was finally transferred to the large flowered form. Years of self-pollination had kept the little orange from becoming a big one and when this habit was broken, so was its problem. I mention this because some amateur hybridizers make the mistake of deliberately self-pollinating which is like a needle stuck in a record going around and around with no chance to get out of the groove.

By no means does this imply that size was paramount in my breeding program. Like Gertrude Jekyll, I saw only coarseness in size for the sake of size, but when accompanied by a graceful carriage it then adds to the whole. I can remember no instance, other than the orange polyanthus, where size was the goal. Rather it took care of itself since size naturally increases with cross-pollination. And, too, when selecting parent stock the largest was instinctively chosen, all other characteristics being equal. Substance, one of the most desirable qualities, was also a free-will offering. Without it a spring garden flower cannot remain calm and unruffled under the beatings of rain and hail. It is also part of its beauty program, the thick petal texture in itself a sign of refinement which, as time goes on, brings a special glow to a flower—a clarity of tone, a brilliance or a hot sheen, a pool of color deep enough to drown in.

But fragrance! That exquisite completion of a flower had to be worked for. The polyanthus has numerous ancestors—the stalkless, variously colored primroses from the Mediterranean, the pale yellow primroses from the hedgerows, copses and streamsides of Britain, and the stalked yellow cowslips and oxlips from the meadows there. Of these, as far as I know, only the cowslip is deeply scented. In the melting pot from which the polyanthus has emerged, the cowslip's heady fragrance was all but lost. As time went on I was occasionally stopped by an indescribable perfume and, other points permitting, these plants were put in the starred rows to spread this added delight throughout the strain. It is cowslip fragrance and more. From somewhere other fragrances came to blend with it and capture the very essence of a sunny May morning in the country.

The temptation to tell you the full measure of ecstasies I have known must be set aside. I would not know where to begin or where to end. How the rich, heavily gold-rimmed chocolate, coffee, and cocoa Spice shades had, by 1953, been developed from the Grand Canyon series; and how the Desert Sunsets, also mothered by the Grand Canyons, overwhelmed me with their sparkling pastels of coral, salmon, apricot and burnt orange. There was the triumph in 1958 of the hardy pink-pink polyanthus developed from the alien one admitted in 1947, so beautiful, so lovely, but too delicate to survive. Ten years it took to breed out its inherited weak constitution and transfer its ethereal wild rose, apple blossom, raspberry and other true pink shades to the robust Barnhaven strain of New Pinks.

Then how many more years to eliminate the mousey-pink shades from the stalkless, acaulis primroses and replace them with these true pinks but with the stalks bred out. When first I saw the loveliness of these Candy Pinks—frosted confections blooming under a sheet of ice in an alder grove next to beds of purest blues—I stood before them crying, the beauty too much to bear.

There are others, so many others that must be passed over but I cannot help mentioning the opulent Victorian shades of plum, violet, mauve, old rose and American Beauty, edged with silver. Exotic lavenders smoked with gray or frosted with sepia, and other shades and colors of that satin and velvet period. But the most riveting, considered the outstanding polyanthuses of all time, is the Barnhaven Cowichan strain begun in 1942. Eyeless, no yellow center to lessen the depth of the bottomless well of smouldering lustrous garnet, violet, amethyst and ultramarine; hot pink-reds, mandarin-and strawberry-reds, based on the New Pinks, often with a coal-black thumb print at the base of the petals—a layering of blue colored cells under the petals' skin. Certainly they are all together unbelievably, extravagantly beautiful beyond describing.

For all the great impact the Cowichans made on the primrose world, the double primroses made even greater. Still the doubles took far less time. There were two planned programs over a period of 8 years—the first, 1957–1961 for 75% doubling; the second, 1961–1965 for 25%. It was the vigorous and colorful progeny of the second program that was hailed as one of the horticultural events of the century. Until then the few doubles generally grown in collectors' gardens were the white, lavender and yellow of English antiquity, a few old Scottish and Irish, and the 100-year-old "Marie Crousse" of French descent. These were all clones of the original plants, the extra petals having displaced the seed-bearing organs. It was a matter of finding now and then, if it was a lucky day, a few specks of pollen hiding deep down in the ruffles and using it on the chosen singles.

I began both programs by using the pollen of the silver-edged, magenta Marie Crousse to impregnate the singles of my choice which colors, of course, were fixed and dominant. And in both programs the first generation bloomed exactly as it should—all singles in a motley of colors. These singles, happily heavy with pollen, were pollinated together in program #2. The second generation of program #2 also behaved as it should: roughly

25% double blooms in pure pinks, French-and cornflower-blues, rich crimsons, scarlet, yellows and bewitching blends ornamented, for the most part, with silver edges inherited from the double parent. Morever, another 25% or so of the second generation that had bloomed single, fully doubled the following spring and remained double which is against the Law. In program #1 the first generation singles were back-crossed with Marie Crousse pollen which gave 75% doubles in the second generation, as it should, but the progeny lacked vigor, size, and aristocratic bearing. Today, however, with many thousands of sturdy, double parents to choose from instead of one, back-crossing for 75% doubling might prove rewarding.

The first flowering of plan #2's second generation produced 340 magnificently robust plants with fully double flowers, ranging in size from a 50¢ piece to a dollar, held erect on stiff stems above the plants—60–135 buds and camellia-like blooms on each with a rich violet scent. But this was only the beginning. For the past 20 years Barnhaven in England has expanded this 1965 introduction using the pollen from 20 succeeding generations of hardy doubles which has sired every imaginable and unimaginable shade, color and combination. They are often edged, dotted or dusted over with silver, heavily fragrant—what I would give to see the blue-black with the pink middle. These and others still to come are destined to be the cherished keepsakes in gardens of the future.

Perhaps this story of a flower, though greatly abridged, is overlong but primroses have been my life's work and from it may come, if nothing else, a reader's enlightenment as to what heights can be reached. Certainly it tells you that elaborate preparation and previous experience are not necessary. Often I have wondered how I instinctively did it. And I am sure it makes clear that in the first generation cross all the blooms will be starlings, not nightingales. But that when the second generation blooms the nightingales begin to sing and any disenchantment turns to delight and beyond delight as the work progresses. Each of us sees color differently and each must follow his own star. Nature has never yet run out of possibilities and she puts her flower children in your hands as clay in the hands of the potter with all the colors on her palette at your disposal. As perception refines, you will find yourself working on ever larger canvases.

Of course it is impossible to tell you how to accomplish what you visualize in the flower families with which you choose to work. But I can tell you some of the moves to avoid. First, prepare some sort of plan as to what you wish to realize so that years are not wasted by daubing pollen here and there indiscriminately hoping that something good will turn up. Secondly, colors in flowers are not produced as painters mix paint—red crossed with white results in magenta, not pink. Flower colors are broken up with yellow but this usually produces blends. When working for form the pollen parent will realize your objective more quickly than the seed parent. And do not make the mistake of pollinating more than your planting-out space will accommodate. Each pod contains many seeds so it is heartbreaking to find that you have more plants than space in which to plant them.

By now it must be redundantly clear that self-pollination must be guarded against. We know that Nature is cunning and will use whatever trick is necessary to see that a flower is pollinated, one way or another. I have watched, for observation purposes only, the long style (pin-eyed form of primrose bloom with stigma held above the anthers) shrink day by day until it dragged its stigma through the pollen almost half an inch below. So pollen must be used or removed before self-pollination can take place. When pollen did not ripen quickly enough I put the petals bearing it on the soil alongside the plant it was taken from and placed a glass jar over it, the heat and moisture ripening it in a day or two. When there was an overage of very special ripe pollen, I put it in a tightly covered jar and stored it in the cool part of the refrigerator. Contrary to botany books which seem to deal with unrefrigerated pollen only, it remained viable for a week or more and was used as stigmas matured.

How long pollen remains potent under refrigeration when not attached to petals, which mold, I cannot say. But I do know that lily pollen from early summer varieties, shaken into labeled vials and refrigerated until the late summer varieties bloomed, is responsible for the mid-summer varieties which have long been on the market. The anthers of the lily candidates for pollination were removed when the pollen was still immature and the flowers bagged. The stigmas, as they matured, were dipped into the refrigerated vials, each plant labeled with the cross made, and re-bagged. The flowers were kept bagged as long as necessary to avoid chance visits from natural pollinators since crosses, in this kind of hybridizing program, must be reliably accurate.

This information may be of use or adapted to your program and also answer the question of when bagging is necessary. Your work may require careful record keeping but do not do more pollinating on paper than in the flesh. If you join, or belong to, a flower society which publishes members' hybridizing methods there is a great deal of pleasure to be had from a shared interest. But methods should be sifted to avoid misinformation often resulting from amateur enthusiasm.

Your last and perhaps most important step concerns picking, curing, and storing the seeds. Since an immature seed cannot germinate, each pod must be picked separately as it shows signs of ripeness, usually changing from green to tan or brown and cracking. I still use brown paper bags, usually #4 but #2 when pods are few. Before picking begins, write the name of the cross on each bag which will be used for subsequent pickings. Never fill a bag more than ⅓ full to avoid mildew, and never pick wet pods. Each bag is twisted tightly at the top, tied with a string long enough to suspend it a foot or two from lines strung in a dry room, preferably an airy one.

Occasionally shake the bags to ensure pod separation and air movement. Most of the seeds will have fallen free from the placentas in a matter of weeks so when the bags are emptied, separately, into a colander, they fall so beautifully, so promisingly plump, into the dish below. The seeds are poured into labeled cellophane packets, put into a tightly covered glass jar, and placed in the refrigerator at around 40°F. The husks are returned to their individual bags and hung to further dry. The next shelling will yield much less seed after which they must be worked by hand to remove the fearful ones still clinging to the placentas, now shrivelled and hard as stone, dead since the ripening.

Hopefully this background, for that is all it is, has opened the door on prospects that will stand you in good stead for many years. For me, this work has been the very subsoil of happiness. And when my personal weather turned stormy it cushioned the blows. You will find a new world in this flower festival of your own making, a world lighted by perceptions that come as quickly as blinking an eye—all in your own backyard.

BARNHAVEN IN OREGON — FROM BARN TO CHALET

13
The Lovers

I once saw a bumblebee resting in the throat of a snapdragon with his hind legs hanging over the lip. I thought at the time how he and I, like all the rest of the million species sharing this planet, grow weary in our daily rounds of gathering food and finding shelter. And then I thought how we presume when we think that our higher intelligence exempts us from the laws governing our linked existence. Flowers cover our crumbling graveyards and ruins. Butterflies hang on the poppies blooming over our battlefields, and the wind brushes and pollinates the grains and other grasses growing there. After every major debacle, from the beginning of flowering life to the present, the species righting themselves with gentle persistence have been plants and their insect partners.

The first flower to bloom on earth was insignificant and wind pollinated but it changed our planet to the same extent as the most cataclysmic upheaval. Its small softness emerged with the emerging spines of the great mountain chains of the world and the chalk cliffs building on the south coast of England. As great blocks of time dropped into the unknown, flowers grew bolder and began advertising in color and scent that they had produced a new food called nectar. Then, somehow, out of the pulsing jelly of creation, various insects materialized to feed on it and, in the feeding, pollinated the flowers. In the soft strength of this survival pact the insects and flowers multiplied in numbers and kinds, dinosaurs and flying reptiles disappeared, and creatures of higher form began to inherit the earth.

Animal life, as we know it, and human life evolved because plants had advanced to the level of caring for their young. After flowering and impregnation plants carried their embryos in cases and packed each case with high energy food. And though the food was stored in the seed case only to nourish the infant plant until established in soil and sun, the seed surplus was great enough to feed and foster the advancing forms of animal life. Many millions of years went into the development of color, scent, and nectar and, as life climbed to ever higher plateaus, flowers assumed more complicated shapes needing specialized agents to pollinate them.

In a simple bunch of flowers we hold the evidence of that great silent explosion of flowering plants, so incomprehensibly sudden, spreading so rapidly over the earth some 25–40 million years ago. Hundreds of millions of years before their coming the planet was altogether monotonously green— first the little mosses and ferns fringing the rivers and lakes followed by the cycads (palm-like plants) and gigantic ferns, all falling before the first winter of the world. Out of this catastrophe a scrubby growth began to cover the bare bones of the earth and the first conifers began to push up, their origin believed to have been passed from the giant seed-ferns before they died as a torch is passed in a run, never dropping. A new line was begun, destined to help clothe our everyday world.

Only a short time before the earth's flowering—who knows how many milliion years—the grasses erupted and began to cover the naked soil, securing it, holding it tightly in its green fingers. It was the grasses that first carried their seeds in cases, and soon the flesh-eaters began to decrease and the modern birds and gentle grazers began to develop, feeding on the protein in the seeds instead of on one another. And doubtless it was a grass that heralded the coming of the true flowers, an insignificant but valiant grass-flower in its first timid trying to light up a totally green world. Then it was that some colossal intelligence set about formulating nectar to lure into being the insects that would be needed for the flowers' sexual survival, all strung out in a sequence of legendary periods of time.

Our minds cannot encompass geological time which is measured by periods of one hundred million years in the four-billion-year-old history of our planet. Or the phenomenon of our sun conjured out of a hydrogen cloud 93 million miles away. It was indeed a very long journey that our simple little bunch of flowers had to make up the evolutionary ladder, rung by precarious rung, to gladden our hearts with its color and sweet scent, and to give us the world as we know it today.

Had that prehistoric world known anything of fragrance it would have been the pungent incense of the conifers which we have come to love as the very essence of Christmas. These trees of ancient lineage, some majestic, others twisted and gnarled, are called conifers because of their woody cone-flowers. They are also called the naked-seeded plants (gymnosperms) because their cones—sometimes only half an inch, sometimes nearly 2 feet—do not offer the sanctuary that our modern flowering plants (angiosperms) provide with their encased placentas. The conifers also pack the fertility of their race into soft pollen-bearing cones, singly or in clusters depending upon the species. They are not often seen unless watched for since they last but a few days in the spring or early summer when their phantom lover, the

wind, is ready and strong and the day is dry.

I have seen such thumb-like fleshy cones on my line of pines that break the western sea-wind, noticed them in passing because of an unfamiliar bit of bright red erecting on the branch tips. From them a golden cloud of pollen billowed for a few days toward my pine grove and when the wind, in that short time, had loosed from the spongy fingers their millions upon millions of dusty grains, the ephemeral little cones shriveled and dropped from the branches. If necessary, the wind could easily carry the pollen to the pines in the mountains many miles away—even as far as 400 miles, for neither the wind nor the surge of fecundity it carries can be held in a net.

Because the right pollen grain must find the right stigma or fail in its mission, all wind-carried pollen must be infinitesimally small, light and dry, and produced in reckless quantities planned for squandering in this hit or miss search for a mate somewhere. It cannot, like flower pollen, be gluey or the clumps would fall like grains of sand. When pollen grains, measured by conifer standards, are larger than is proper as in my pines and spruce, air sacs have been added to keep them afloat. The wind—the most constant lover of them all needing no enticements of any kind—also services many spring-mating deciduous trees whose leaves fall every autumn. Catkins, swinging on the alders and willows and hazels are a pleasing sight in the early spring, but there are also the oaks, the beeches, elms, chestnuts, walnuts and many others relying upon the wind. Nature maintains a tight control over the fecund dispersal holding it until the air is dry, releasing it before too many leaves have emerged to block the pollen in its searching flight.

The conifers, which we affectionately lump together as evergreens (because they keep their needle or scale-like leaves for two or more years, some pines for 15 years, before shedding) grip and hold us for one reason or another. We all have a special feeling for them because of the Christmas connection, and for their aristocratic individualism in gardens, cities and towns, mountains, meadows and deserts. To this I add my abiding respect, even reverence, for their antiquity, their will to endure where no other plant would even try. Their longevity is partly due to the fact that they are not ashamed to bow head and limb before the elements so they break less under pressure than the unbending broad-leaved hardwoods.

Of the 7 conifer families with their 550 species, the pines and firs are best known in the Pacific Northwest. Northern California's great Ponderosa

Pine forests are apt to be passed by in the pilgrimage to the ancient Sequoias wearing their age in hallowed splendor. There are but two species left, the redoubtable Sequoia with its scale-like sprays—the Big Tree of the Sierra Nevadas—and its close relative, the Redwood of the coast with its sprays of flat needles. The coastal brother, encouraged in its growth by the warmth and rain, is the taller—one being the tallest tree in the world holding its head 364 feet into the sky.

The Redwoods' mountain kin has grown bulkier and tougher defending itself with buttressed base and scales for leaves against the freezing winds of winter and the dry summers. One, General Sherman, is considered the largest living thing, a colossus standing on a foundation 36½' through having accumulated, so far, between 3,500 and 4,000 years. His ancestors watched the prehistoric monsters take their final leave and witnessed the coming of the first butterfly, moth, beetle and bee though unable to enter into a sexual relationship with them. It is said that they cannot die, these Sequoias which have carried the Cherokee scholar's name now for more than 100 years. And that no insect, fungus or fire can reach the heart of them because of the protective bark that is more than a foot through. Only the saw brings them to a crashing end.

Reproduction goes on among these California giants despite age and remarkably small cones for the wind to find. In contrast, there are stunted conifers of hoary age, twisted this way and that in their determination to survive at timberline, whose bristly cones may reach 3½''. These are the Bristlecone Pines fighting an endless battle in the hostile territory of the Southwest's desert mountains. Only those enthusiasts fortunate enough to know their two-mile-high location and willing to climb the merciless wind— sometimes too strong for standing, sometimes in summer snow—can marvel firsthand at the unconquerable Bristlecones. In comparison, General Sherman has grown old in luxury.

These skyline Bristlecones, mauled by freezing winds, scoured by sandblasts and scalded by the sun, are invincible. They endure long periods of starvation and thirst when the snows do not melt for several summers, when minerals and water are locked away in the rock-strewn terrain beneath. No growth can be made then and in the good years there are but three months in which to try. So it is impossible to determine how much older some of these intrepid trees are than the 4,000 years allotted them. They can hope to reach 40–50' but some, which have grown nearly 6', have had to

struggle more than 900 years to do it in this barren environment. One dwarf of 2', possibly 50 years old, was seen bearing one cone bristling defiance at a relentless world in its indomitable will to mate though ravished by a wind out of control.

Not much has been said about the Bristlecone Pines. They are not meant to be found, their exact locations generally withheld hoping to protect them from souvenir hunters. Some have established themselves in valleys at lower elevations and seed-bearing cones have been taken to nurseries for propagation. From there the seedling trees have settled into a life of ease in collectors' plantings but these have lost the majestic stoicism necessary to survive in stark circumstances. They are just another pine, fast growing in kindly climates, grown soft with the food and drink always at hand.

No living thing on this planet is more venerable, more worthy of the deepest admiration and respect, than the hardship-hardened Bristlecones. But I do so love the serenity of a Ponderosa forest. Always, on my way over the mountains separating Oregon into the wet and the dry, I stop on the semiarid east slope and make my way into one of the many stands towering there. I walk its polished aisles with the sun slanting down between the trees to the glistening floor of needles and pick up the large fat cones, their seeds shed, for the Christmas mantel. I stand there in the midst of it breathing in the incense of their hatpin leaves, listening to the singing of the wind in their branches, and feel that I am in the noblest of all cathedrals. It is hard to leave the conifers and their intimate alliance with the wind.

When we think of the winged lovers we think of romance and soft bodies, graceful in their wooing, so it is difficult to see a lumbering beetle in the role of suitor. Yet they were the first primitive insects, coming early into the wooden world of conifers whose bark is still home to some of them. And they continue to be attracted to plants of ancient ancestry—the magnolias, peonies and some of the water lilies. I have seen gray beetles and black beetles, some destructive, some not, but the only beetle I have seen fly is the brightly varnished and polka dotted lady bird—the ladybug we cherish for the inroads they make on aphid populations and other sap-sucking insects. Yet beetles have not one but two pairs of wings—the upper pair being horny forewings that cover and protect the soft flight wings should they wish to use them.

Whatever we think of beetles we should not forget that they are hardened survivors of a hard age. That there was no easy life for them until the first flowers produced pollen too sticky for the wind's liking. There still was no nectar, consequently no soft-winged sippers, but the first flowers did produce pollen in quantities large enough to feed the biting beetles in return for the pollinating. Some flowers still curry favor with certain beetles even though they do produce a bit of nectar.

Nectar is the common denominator of the sipping pollinators which, in themselves, could be considered converted nectar—the jaunty, jeweled hummingbirds are said to have been created either out of it or because of it. It provides the tongued lovers' energy; in mythology it was the life-giving drink of the gods; actually it is largely sucrose which we know and use as sugar and is the raw material from which honey is made. A few flowers carry as much as 75% sugar in their nectar but the average is around 30–35%. Nectar is produced by a special gland, is positioned where pollinators must probe for it with their tongue, and is protected from rain and spillage by hidden hairs or in the spurs of such flowers as columbines. I well remember the sweetness in the wild columbines when I picked them in the fields and sucked the nectar from the spurs so long ago.

Just as our fruits and berries have been designed for birds to eat and scatter the seeds, so Nature has embroidered our plants with flowers to entice pollinators to feed and make possible the seeds. Color, scent and form, pollinator, climate and season—all have been entangled with the utmost care. Our early spring flowers with their delicate scents are predominately

yellow and white because the honeybee is earliest out and sees yellow and white as clearly as a sailor sees a beacon. So it is the daffodil and junquil, the snowdrop, English primrose and cowslip, forsythia and jasmine, the plum and all the pale boughs perfumed like an oriental bride that are simply fashioned to attract the bee. In all this sweet flood not a complicated bloom is to be found for the bee must work quickly to gather nectar from some 700 blossoms in an hour.

Though honeybees and bumblebees prefer yellow they can see blue and bluish-purple (also ultraviolet which of course we cannot) and these colors increase as the weather warms. For maximum contrast the majority of blue and off-blue flowers surround their pollen with a conspicuous landing field of yellow, white or cream to guide the pollinators to the nectar with the swiftest accuracy. These nectar guides become more fancy as the spring grows older and the more colorful flowers begin to appear wearing dots, or stripes, or a gold necklace around their throat or, in a flush of artistic endeavor, all patterned on one blossom. When there are no guides, as in the magnolias with large, pale flowers, the bees often lose their way before reaching the center of the bloom. To red the bee is blind, like green it appears

black. So the red flower bent upon enticing bees signals them with the yellow of its pollen and any scent it may carry. The bee tumbling about in a full-blown dark red rose found its way to the unseen flower by the clustered gold of its stamens and the beckoning, voluptuous fragrance of it.

Most gardeners are used to seeing honeybees among their flowers so pay little or no attention to them because they are a common sight, but they may be surprised to learn just how uncommon they are. Granted that in their modest browns and tan they do not catch and hold the eye like butterflies who play more and work less. But honeybees are totally fascinating creatures leading such a highly ordered social life that only bits and pieces of their story can be told in a few pages. Certainly they are the most loyal of the winged lovers in their commitment to the flowers they can see and smell and taste with tongues made for probing all but the deep throated.

Like us, they are naturally partial to sweet tastes, do not mind the bitter as much as we, but we accept the sour and salty more readily than they. Their sense of smell is similar to ours and about as sensitive though their ability to distinguish a certain scent in a knot of fragrances is more highly refined. Unlike color, which guides from a distance, fragrance is a short-range lure to the flower that might otherwise be unseen. Fragrance is mixed with the pollen grains which the bee smells and feels simultaneously with her antennae, or feelers as we rightly call them.

The honeybees we see are the virgins who have graduated from house chores to the outside world of fields and gardens. She collects nectar as quickly as possible, then hurries home gilded over with pollen sticking to her body and stuffed into the baskets on her hind legs. She may have had to work two hours and flown more than a mile before her stomach-tank and baskets were filled and she could return and unload the nectar into special storage cells, or pass it over to a younger virgin. She then rubs off the pollen into cells made for its storage and is out and foraging again unless she has found an area particularly rich in pollen and nectar. In such case she performs a dance—sometimes simple, other times intricate in our eyes—born of an intelligence that has been diverging from ours for half a billion years and more.

Her choreography relates to distance and flight direction and is simple if the source lies, say, within a radius of 300 feet from the hive. If so, it is a round dance, a sort of ring-around-a-rosy performed in the darkness of the hive on the vertical face of the honeycomb with her sister workers following closely in her steps. They are further guided by the scent of the flowers she has visited, the food she has brought, and the scent she left behind her like a ribbon tied on a bush.

But if the source lies much beyond this range, her dance becomes a complicated bit of arithmetic forming a figure-of-eight. She communicates direction by the location of the sun—straight up the comb means to head directly for it, straight down directly away from it, diverging angles indicate right or left. As she points out location, she signals distance by the speed of her dance—the greater the distance the slower the dance—and by the number of times she wags her body having taken into account a head wind that hinders flight or a tail wind that helps.

The virgin worker is 10 days old when she goes into the fields where she labors perhaps a month before she dies. In those first 10 days she worked indoors, obeying without question the "spirit of the hive"—work and work only for the common good governed by thrift and prudence to provide food for all whatever the season. The colony is a highly advanced society in which the adolescent females nurse and tend the young, feeding them the baby food called beebread made with pollen and nectar or honey. They wait upon the queen, air or heat the hive by fanning their wings and, if necessary, evaporate excess water from the honey. There are wax-makers, welders, chemists to preserve the honey, capsule-makers to seal the cells when the honey is ripe. There is a maintenance detail to keep the hive clean and remove the dead whose hive life may have been 5 or 6 months. And a police force to guard the entrance, barricading it if marauders cannot be frightened away.

There are also the architects and masons who design and construct the precise hexagonal cells that make up the comb. The spirit of the hive regulates the size and number of these cells—small and many for workers, large and few for the males, or drones, still larger and fewer for the queen and princesses. It decrees day by day how many virgin workers will be hatched based on the number of flowers in bloom. It determines sex—the working females from fertilized eggs, all unable to mate; the drones from unfertilized eggs whose work will be over when one is chosen to mate with and impregnate the queen on her nuptial flight. The corpulent queen lives and lays eggs of one kind or another for 3–5 years. All continue on their appointed rounds as a matter of course, day after day without cease, throughout the spring, summer and fall in a civilization that surely must be the best ordered in the animal world outside our own.

Bumblebees, unlike their honeybee cousins, live a hand-to-mouth life having no hive, storing no honey but, to me, are delightfully amusing in a number of ways. Despite their pompous look, under a magnifying glass they have the face of a fuzzy rabbit, their wings attached in such a way as to appear like long ears laid back. Seen among the flowers, the bumbler is a handsome creature, much larger than the honeybee and with pretensions to style and dash in her shining black fur jacket, cream or orange bustle, gold collar and gold leg-muffs stuffed with pollen for beebread.

The bumblebee queen shops carefully to find a home as comfortable as the one in my carport woodpile. One queen decided to settle there last spring after emerging from her underground burrow where she spent most of the fall and the entire winter hibernating after her early autumn wedding. The nest in the woodpile has been empty now since mid-September when I missed them and knew that the queen, old by then, her daughters and any remaining males, had died or hibernated. I cannot expect to see a young queen shopping until next spring when the temperature is around 50° F and the sun has warmed the lot of them out of the earth's pockets. But I do hope

THE BEES' WOODPILE

one will decide to come and rear her smallish family there and let me watch their daily life another year. When I invaded their privacy they warned me but did not sting because I carried no antagonizing odor of fear.

The bumblebee's length of tongue, more than half an inch, allows them to probe nectaries beyond the reach of the shorter-tongued honeybee. I can still hear that joyous shout of a pansy seed grower, "the bumblers are here!", for without them my friend would have been out of business then and there. But many flowers offer a gathering place for both lovers who arrive together, equally eager, at exactly a given time.

I find it strange that flower at least some of them, produce nectar only at certain times of the day or have a peak nectar flow which must be caught. When I learned that honeybees visit blue cornflowers in the morning at 11 o'clock and again in the afternoon at 3, I checked for a number of days and found both cousins working the same flower head at exactly these times. But only the central portion since the outer florets are meant for signaling so carry no nectar.

I also thought it strange that a honeybee and a bumblebee sipping from the same cornflower cup were friendly but fought with their own kind. And that this mateship between the cousins, just as the hostility among themselves, extended to the neighboring Iceland poppies. Neither bee is influenced by the tilt of the sun's shawl. This timing intelligence, like the directional dance, has been acquired over the eons needed to develop from a carnivorous wasp-like creature to a highly educated vegetarian living on the pollen and nectar flowers produce for their own survival.

Often in the summer I have revived with sugar water many an exhausted bumblebee and honeybee trapped indoors. With them I felt as one always feels when saving a life, but to hold an exhausted hummingbird is to have held for that short time a scintillating fragment of illusion. Then it was my heart that beat fast with anxiety as I carried from the house one of these exquisite creatures, inert and light as a puff of dandelion seed. Yet each time life quickened, and always there was the wonder of its tongue.

More than an inch long, it flicked out from the darning needle bill to the spoon of dissolved sugar again and again with the speed of a spring tightly coiled and suddenly released. Few have seen a hummingbird's tongue, few know they have one held in reserve to reach the nectaries of the most deep-throated flowers. I am sure that had it been necessary even more tongue could have been loosed as it lay, prone, in my hand. And always recovery was the same—the feeding, the resting a minute or so, the cool searching look into my eyes, then suddenly gone—this splendid, heart-wrenching speck of bird.

Despite seeming fragility it had the spirit and could command the strength to fly here from its Mexican or Central American home to which it will return in a few months. How, when their daily need for food is greater than that of any living thing, can they cruise such a distance at a speed of 35 miles an hour. Those native to tropical South America fly south to their own temperate zone and back each year, for hummingbirds are unique to the Americas.

There are other pollinating birds in other lands—the Hawaiian honeycreepers, and the sweet singing honey eaters and certain small parrots I have seen working in tropical Australia. But in Europe there are no indigenous pollinating birds since none are needed for the typically simple flowers native to its temperate climate. There the bee is the dominant lover in the alliance between flower and pollinator but, when hummingbird flowers are transplanted to non-hummingbird country, the bees consummate the marriage with difficulty or, more likely, not at all.

Red is hummingbird color, so summer flares with brilliant flowers often elaborately designed and as often unscented since hummingbirds care little or nothing for fragrance. It almost seems that Nature in her calculated thrift seldom splashes the more sophisticated, resplendent flowers with perfume knowing that they will be serviced without it. So the little bird's sense of smell is not keen but their vision is sharp and farsighted—blue and purple being secondary to red which draws them like a moth to the flame. There is a hummingbird who comes to my kitchen window again and again to eye the bowl of red roses on the table 10 feet away. It seems not to move as it hangs in mid-air 3 inches from the glass for half a minute each visit before realizing the flowers are beyond reach.

Hummingbird flowers have a passion for self-advertisement, flaunting themselves in showy colors and fancy forms as the fuchsias do to attract the bird born to be their lover. Like many flowers relying upon hummingbirds for their continuance, fuchsias have no landing platform since none is needed for these minute acrobats to reach the nectar. They stand on air before the blossom, wings humming as they whir more than 3,000 beats a minute to keep them suspended before it, or to lift themselves straight up, or to suddenly go into reverse before darting away.

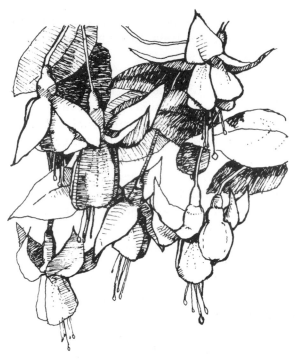

So great is their need to keep their engine fueled they must work thousands of blooms a day for the quick energy nectar gives and for the pollen that provides protein. And they must also pick off as many insects as can be found for additional protein just to stay alive until evening grays the flowers. Then they return to their secret place to hibernate through the night just as larger animals hibernate through the winter. It must be a place safe from all things and from hands that could pick them off the bough like an ornament and do what they wished with them. Every morning, just before first light when their body temperature begins to rise again, I hear the one who overnights in the tall, bushy rhododendron outside my bedroom window squeak like a mouse. In this small sound is the joy of finding himself alive again, knowing that soon there will be light enough to go out into his world of color and work another day.

It was at Barnhaven that I first realized these incredible flyers are mini-bombers loaded with Latin excitability, even belligerence, and entirely without fear. There were times—when they and I wanted to pollinate the same brilliant red Cowichan polyanthus—that I had to shield my eyes from repeated attacks as I kept brushing them away. Here, on the coast, they delight me with their love of play, bounding in unison on the spray from the hose or playing tag in the water. Then sitting in the sun on the telephone wire, preening their feathers dry for a few minutes before they dash to a nearby fuchsia, its scarlet earrings dangling in cascades from the eaves.

Of the 10 hummingbird species that follow the flowers as they bloom across the western states, only two come to the Pacific Northwest—the Rufous and the Anna. It is the Rufous with jade cap and ruby muffler who make their spring and summer home with me and, recently, some have stayed several winters though temperatures dropped into the low 20s. So I keep my feeder well filled with a thin syrup—3 parts distilled water to 1 part sugar (the nectar formula of hummingbird flowers) to which I add 1 or 2 drops of red coloring to guide them. I hang it conspicuously in the Japanese quince in early fall leaving it there until late spring when bloom is plentiful again. Their fresh insect protein hangs in the spiderwebs constantly being spun under the eaves of this old house. When the weather warms, the webs will be used to line their nests with gossamer nothingness. Not everyone has the pleasure of watching these high-spirited, highly intelligent pollinators go about their daily life but I wish it could be so.

In the flower world honeybees are the ultra-responsible, quiet Quakers; hummingbirds, the flashy but responsible madcaps; butterflies, the irresponsible jet setters born to flit, court and couple, and to bask in the sun. Perhaps their life is given over to more idling than work because it is so short and so precarious. They are not early up in the morning to go nectaring and pollinating for several reasons. One, they are not as dependent upon flowers as are the others. They enjoy tippling on the juices of fermenting fruit, syphoning on a pile of fresh manure or around a pool of urine, gathering around mud puddles for the salts there—a sort of club for dawdling and communication.

Without their artful wings, butterflies would be as drab as flying ants. It is their silken wings, tie-and-dye colorings with catchy designs which fascinate us. Yet, actually, their four wings are without color as we know it, and the designs on them are purely protective devices produced in the magical process of decoration. Millions of overlapping scales shingle the wings, pigmented but unseen in some species, entirely without pigmentation in others. Those carrying concealed pigments in their scales produce the soft earth colors, and black, white, yellow, and orange by absorbing or reflecting the light's play and distance. The scales on the scintillating, highly colored wings are ridged, 3-dimensional and devoid of all pigments—their sapphire, emerald or amethyst hues produced by the refraction and reflection of light as in the making of a rainbow.

Those decorative circles and dots, patches and patterns on butterfly wings are called eyespots and are there not to embellish the painting but to trick the birds. They act as deflecting targets should a bird strike—a pierced wing is better than being swallowed alive. They also help to camouflage, deceiving the birds into thinking it a flower or that it is not there at all. And the designs are dappled in such a way as to remind the birds of foods distasteful to them by imitating the look of the unpleasant meal. Certainly no method of survival has been evolved that can even approach the artfulness of painting without paint on a butterfly wing.

Still there is more to these fanciful wings than meets the eye. The front pair plays a vital part in sexual survival by means of scent scales which, upon demand, emit a delightful flowery fragrance (perfumed hormones) to make sure that male and female are of the same species and, if so, to sexually excite the female. But first there is the dance he performs facing his partner— the dance of his species with its own courtly and complex set of movements—a getting-to-know-you visual appraisal. If all is well, the male atomizes the air with his powerful blend of glandular perfume for the closer communication of smell and allure. He ends with a low bow before her, front wings pushed close to her feelers so she can smell and smell again the irresistible aphrodisiac until she is totally lost.

Then, with her power of sex determination, the egg laying begins followed by the hatching and caterpillar stage. The caterpillars, upon eating their fill of leaves, retire to the protection of the cocoon where organs mysteriously rearrange themselves into entirely new shapes and functions. At last there emerges from the worm a fairy prince or princess. And always the males appear first, eagerly awaiting the females—so eagerly that virginity seldom survives the morning of emergence.

Over their long evolvement butterflies instinctively concluded that their chief concern must be the reproduction of their kind as quickly and as abundantly as possible. All come into the world with the mark of sadness upon them for, even without accident, the adult of most species averages only about two weeks in which to cram all their living and loving. As always there are exceptions—notably the Monarchs who may have come from as far north as Canada to hibernate in the trees of their favorite West Coast wintering place at Pacific Grove on California's Bay of Monterey. They remind me of stained glass pieces—large orange wings barred and veined with black, edged in black with white polka dots—hanging in clumps or festooned from branch to branch. There they drowse and wait for the milkweeds' call to rouse themselves and fly north again and lay their eggs in the hospitality they offer.

At the other end of the spectrum are the very delicate species whose hold on life may last but two days. Between these extremes are those who try to overwinter in the niches and crannies of the gardens they sheltered in during spring and summer nights. Some survive to visit early flowering plants and shrubs but first there must be enough sun in which to bask and warm themselves before they have the power to fly. It is the same in all seasons when chill rides the air, so when you see butterflies basking you know they are sunning themselves to raise body and flight muscle temperatures.

Butterfly population is determined more by climate with its day-to-day weather than by the flowers they prefer. Spring and summer winds and rain take as heavy a toll as predators for their wings are their Achilles heel. If there is enough sun to warm them into action a sudden gust could drive them into twigs or other sharp objects where they might hang, helpless, or be too badly torn to fly again. This is the reason butterflies are less numerous in species and count on the cool and windy Northwest and Northeast coasts than in warmer, less windy areas. Many will not leave their retreat in cloudy weather and even if the day is warm, should a cloud float over and shade them, or a storm threaten, they hurry back to shelter.

There is a headland here just north of my enchanted meadow with its own flowered field overlooking the sea. Pines and spruce approach it from the east but stop short as though by command. Here, on this high meadow, flocks of butterflies—copper-and-black, white, and intense blue—hover over the wild flowers crouching in the grass. Against all reason they inhabit this promontory, flying only a short way out from the sheltering woods to nectar on sunny windless days returning quickly when need be. Perhaps this is their birthplace and one generation after another has learned to adapt to the coast's wayward ways.

I doubt that butterflies are as fussy about flowers as some would have us believe except their fatuous love for Buddleias, commonly called the Butterfly Bush because its light, honey-like fragrance is impossible to resist. There is such a bush across the street and I have watched from only a foot away an Admiral unroll almost an inch of tongue from its coil between his eyes and probe floret after floret packed tightly into racemes. As he draws up the thin, sweet liquid his feet are tasting it at a rate 150 times keener than our keenest taste buds could know.

Other butterflies visit the Shasta daisies and the pink phlox and other open flowers with nectaries easily reached. Butterfly sight is sharp but short, seeing the colors we see; smelling as we smell but only at a short distance since fragrance is relatively unimportant to them excepting that of the siren Buddleia. They cruise at random for flowers and mates stopping to hover and investigate every likely colored object they see until the summer begins to cool. Then the flowers begin to drift back to more spring-like types for the honeybees who work through the year's final flowering.

Various species of butterflies have developed an affinity for flowers of both temperate and tropical zones, flower and pollinator accommodating one another to satisfy mutual needs. In the jungles of north Queensland and in Papua/New Guinea (separated from Australia by an eighty-mile-wide strait) there are no honeybees as in the temperate zone, and no humming-birds as in the Americas. So the large, dramatically colored, unscented flowers commonly thrust their sexual parts well above the petals for the butterflies to hover over and fertilize.

Scarlet, pink, and rose hibiscus are everywhere. And on the wet New Guinea side of the island, vines with large neon blue flowers, which can only be described as a cross between a morning-glory and a sweet pea, drape everything from the coast to the highlands. And hovering over them are the fabulously large, flashing blue Ulysses Swallowtails. This big island is home to the largest butterflies in the world—one species almost a foot across—and the most beautiful. Yet inhabitants are quite casual about them as they fly around on wings of lavender, gold, blue, iridescent green and amethyst combinations.

One late afternoon I stood transfixed before a mountainous Bougainvillaea watching hundreds of blue Swallowtails fluttering about a solid front of flourescent pink bracts. I knew that the display would soon end since night drops swiftly there extinguishing the vivid flowers and sending the butterflies to bed. It is then that the long-tongued moths wake and visit the white flowers drenching the air with seductive fragrances to guide them—coffee blossoms and their gardenia cousins, and the white tubes of bouvardia, all spilling the perfumed languor of the tropics from a height of 10 feet and more. But of all the nighttime flowers the Plumeria with its aphrodisiac perfume, its softly rounded star-shape and full-bodied petals, is by the far the most haunting. This is the Frangipani of the South Pacific and its moon color and sensual fragrance lure adventurers and writers as well as moths. It is the enchantress of the evening and the mistress of the night, and morning finds its blossoms lying, fulfilled, on every footpath.

But it is not always moon colored and sensuously scented for in the tropics the pollinators and flowers dance to the rain's tune. I found that on the drier Papuan side of the island's dividing range most of the frangis were pale and heavily perfumed but there were also some pink and light rose. From these a genteel, lemony-spice scent rose to freshen the night. On the eastern side of the mountains, where some 300″ of rain fall annually, frangis develop into gracefully awkward small trees with flowers of deepening color and lessening fragrance. Among them are the blood-reds with no fragrance and little beauty except for the great, shocking blue Swallowtails covering them, more flower than the flower itself.

Thinking back makes me wonder if, subconsciously, I patterned my 100′ x 100′ piece of land here after that remote island plantation off the Solomons where the soil was never idle and whose Chinese owner tolerated no waste. Where I could leisurely observe his money-making, soil-making, space-saving program on land he took from the jungle and transformed it to serried rows of cacaos and coconuts to shade them. Certainly there are no rainbowed lorikeets or electric-blue butterflies here to remind me of it. The beach I walk is often a monochrome of soft grays and white—gray and white gulls floating in a gray sky, gray and white sandpipers running without movement at the edge of a gray and white sea.

The shrubs and trees here are not so richly perfumed but my purple leaf plum fills me with an exquisite tenderness throughout the seasons. In late February it hides its nakedness in filmy pink, and as the buds open and spill their musky scent over the courtyard I remember that in the Orient plum blossoms personify young love and embody immortality. I see the plum tree every time I look up from this work which, because of its ever-expanding vistas, has occupied me through numerous leafings and sheddings. As time passed I began to experience it as well as to see it. Now when the wind scatters its blossoms over the lawn I know why the ceremonial hand in a tea garden shakes a plum bough over his diminutive plot of grass to perfect the perfection of it. Now I see a deeper meaning in the fiery leaves of its youth imperceptibly mellowing to the polished mahogany of age—then the falling, the resting, the flowering, and the leafing again.

In the natural world nothing exists alone or without reason. Everything is as well-ordered and unified in one place as another. The cacao trees and my purple leaf plum renew themselves in the same way according to the rhythm dictated by their environment. The recyclers and the other soil families and the pollinators all work together, there as here, toward the same end. Nature is more lavish there but what she gives with one hand she takes back with the other for the good of all.

As this book progressed and I was drawn deeper and deeper into the nobility of life on every benign level, the more personal my involvement became. Never is this feeling of oneness and ongoingness with the living earth stronger than when my hands are in the soil. And now that I am rich with still another spring the desk can hold me no longer. With the soil warming and drying under an April sun I need it as urgently as it needs me so I am going out to cultivate it and the habit of quiet happiness.

the end

Bibliography

1. *Our Living Soil.* Cook, J. Gordon (Fellow of the Royal Institute of Chemistry) The Dial Press. 1960. New York.

2. *Western Fertilizer Handbook.* Published and distributed by Soil Improvement Committee California Fertilizer Association, 1968. Sacramento, California.

3. *Handbook on Soils.* Brooklyn Botanic Garden Record, published by Brooklyn Botanic Garden, 1966. Baltimore, Maryland

4. *Soil Fertility.* Gardener, Hugh (Extension Soils Specialist, Oregon State University) OSU

5. *Botany.* Wilson, Carl L. (Professor of Botany, Dartmouth College), and Loomis, Walter E. (Professor of Botany, Iowa State College). The Dryden Press, 1958. New York

6. *Life, An Introduction to Biology.* Simpson, George Gaylord, Columbia University. Pittendrigh, Colin S., Princeton University. Tiffany, Lewis H., Northwestern University. Harcourt, Brace and Company, 1957. New York

7. *Plant Growth.* Yocum, L. Edwin (Professor of Botany, The George Washington University). The Jaques Cattel Press, 1945. Lancaster, Pennsylvania.

8. *Great Men of Modern Agriculture.* Cannon, Grant G. (Editor, The Farm Quarterly). The Macmillan Company. 1963. New York

9. *The Sea Around Us.* Carson, Rachel. Oxford University Press. 1961. New York

10. *Gardening Without Work.* Stout, Ruth The Devin-Adair Company, 1970. Old Greenwich, Connecticut.

11. *Let's Get Well.* Davis, Adelle Harcourt, Brace & World, Inc., 1965. New York

12. *The Living Garden.* Salisbury, E. J. (D. Sc., F.R.S.) The Macmillan Company, 1936. New York

13. *The Immense Journey.* Eiseley, Loren Vintage Books (Random House), 1946–1957. New York

14. *Flowering Earth.* Peattie, Donald Culross. G. P. Putnam's Sons, 1939. New York

15. *George Forrest.* Published by The Scottish Rock Garden Club, 1935. Edinburgh, Scotland

16. *Genetics.* Winchester, A. M. (John B. Stetson University) Houghton Mifflin Company, 1951

17. *Burbank: A Gardener Touched With Genius The Life of Luther Burbank.* Dreyer, Peter Coward, McCann & Geoghegan, Inc. N.Y. and Longman Canada, Ltd. Toronto, 1975

18. *The Hive and the Honey Bee.* (Edited by Dadant & Sons with the collaboration of a Staff of Specialists) Dadant & Sons, Hamilton, Illinois (Publishers of the American Bee Journal)

19. *The Story of Pollination* Meeuse, B. J. D. (University of Washington). The Ronald Press Company, 1961. New York

20. *A Natural History of Western Trees.* Peattie, Donald Culross. Bonanza Books, New York, 1948

21. *The Audubon Society Handbook for Butterfly Watchers.* Pyle, Robert Michael. Charles Scribner's Sons. New York, 1984

22. *Tropical Crops Dicotyledons.* Purseglove, J. W. (University of the West Indies, St. Augustine, Trinidad). The English Language Book Society and Longman, 1968. London

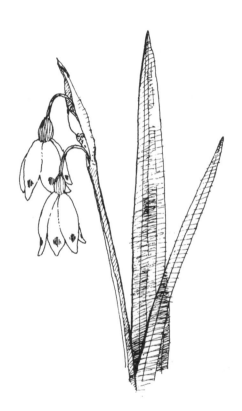